HANDMADE Christians in a Cookie Cutter World

HANDMADE Christians

John Cunyus

Cover design: Kevin Darst

10 9 8 7 6 5 4 3 2 1 97 98 99 00 01 02

Library of Congress Cataloging–in–Publication Data

Cunyus, John.
Handmade Christians in a cookie-cutter world / John Cunyus.
p. cm.
ISBN 0-8272-1426-X
1. Meditations. I. Title.
BV4832.2.C85 1997 97-6718
242—dc21 CIP

Contents

A Word to the Reader

The Apostle Paul usually began his letters with a blessing to his readers: "Grace to you and peace from God our Father and the Lord Jesus Christ." I can't think of a better way to begin a conversation. I certainly pray God's blessing and peace on you as you make your way through these meditations.

These essays grew out of certain basic convictions. I am convinced, first of all, that Jesus Christ is Lord—and that all truth, wherever we find it, reflects Christ's lordship. I try to make that conviction the bedrock of everything I do.

Second, I believe that the ultimate test of Christian faith is in the living of it. Either we realize our share in the kingdom of God here and now or not at all. Since God's presence is joy itself, peace itself, holiness itself, missing out on communion with God is the greatest tragedy a life can suffer. If this work helps just one reader not only hear the good news but live it, I will be satisfied.

Third,I believe that being able to state Christ's truth briefly, accurately, and (I hope) gracefully is supremely important these days. We live in a televised, highly distractible culture that has little patience for long sermons or lengthy perorations. It's a preacher's joke that if you can't be good, at least be brief—and it is my feeling that if you can be both, you are truly blessed. I hope these essays present one view on the heart of the gospel briefly and, if God grants, eloquently.

These meditations are for your use. You may want to use them in your daily devotions, your church school class or small group, or as part of your worship. Whatever you do, though, and whatever I do, may it all be done for the glory of God.

Grace to you, and peace!

John Cunyus

Handmade Christians in a Cookie-Cutter World

Cookie-cutters have their uses. I always like the ones my wife uses at Christmas time: Santa Claus, little reindeer, Christmas trees, and the like. They all come out perfectly, ready to be decorated. There is one form in the batch that I've never quite recognized, sort of a "Rorshach Christmas cookie," but that's because my Christmas cookie I.Q. is lower than average.

The cookie-cutter method works for more than just cookies, too. It's the preeminent hallmark of the industrial age, in my opinion. Consider that in the Middle Ages all horse harnesses, wagons, farm implements, and tools were handmade by individual craftsmen. No doubt many of those harnesses and tools bordered on being works of art, far superior to anything manufactured today. Still, how many could one worker turn out in a given period of time? One a month? Maybe two if she worked fast? No wonder cities were small and famines were frequent.

What we lose in craftsmanship by employing the cookie-cutter method in the making of our tools, modes of transport, and such, we more than make up for in terms of convenience. It might be nice to own handmade tools, but do we really lose much by owning factory-made ones? I don't think so. The relative inelegance of our implements is more than offset by the abundance those implements make possible.

There are places on earth where most things are still handmade. Remember seeing pictures of carved wooden plows in the backdrop of news coverage from various trouble spots around the world? Only the automatic weapons are machine-made in such places, it sometimes seems.

For all its undoubted benefits, the cookie-cutter method has down sides too. For one, it just doesn't apply to all circumstances. Cookie-cutter education in our schools simply doesn't work. While all capable children need to learn to read, write, and calculate, there's not a "one-size-fits-all" formula for teaching them. Different children learn in different ways. Shoving all youngsters into the same mold often does far more harm than good.

Cookie-cutter religion doesn't work either. Some churches, some denominations even, try mightily to stamp all believers out of the same mold. They expect conformity of thought, doctrine, even politics. Yet we can measure how unsuccessful such efforts are by how bitterly such groups condemn and attack those who don't agree with them. In my experience, the louder someone shouts, "My way is the only way," the more insecure they feel inside.

There has been no "industrial revolution" in human spiritual formation. We each need a handmade faith, however automated our world may have become. Why? Because each of us has a unique perspective on divinity. God shares Godself with each of us in ways appropriate to us. While we learn from the faith of others, we are saved finally by our own faith and by no one else's. So the process must be given time, care, and craftsmanship in order to prepare us properly.

I hope that is what we offer one another through our churches. Whatever our church's size, mega-, micro-, or somewhere in between, let's resist the temptation to let them be cookie-cutter congregations where individuals get lost in whatever-sized crowd there is. Let's strive to make them churches where each person matters, where, hopefully, all of us work together to grow into the people God would have us be.

Handmade Christians in a cookie-cutter world. It's kind of a nice idea, isn't it?

SPIRITUAL TODDLING

She took her first steps the other day, her little face as intent as a Spanish explorer setting out for the New World. Mom was the home continent, Dad was the New World, and big sister Martha, watching from the sidelines with just a tinge of jealousy, was the mythical sea-monster to be overcome. But little Gracie made it, toddling on little legs a distance that to us is nothing, but to her meant nothing less than a new dimension of life.

I first thought, watching her stumble from one side to another, that the name "Grace" is not yet entirely accurate. She has a name she'll have to live up to. When we were looking for baby names, I read something about the name John that stuck with me: "If you have to name a kid after a room in the house, why not name him 'Foyer'?" "Grace" really isn't a bad name to try and live up to, all things considered. Physical grace will come, I'm sure, even as the spiritual grace has been here all along.

As this fledgling learns to walk, I realize I can't teach her how to do it. I can encourage her and celebrate her successes. I can set an example for her by walking myself (something I'm quite good at as long as there's no chewing gum involved). I can even comfort her when she falls. But the really hard work she's got to do on her own. She'll take her lumps in the process, but the rewards she'll reap from learning how to do it well will far outweigh the pain involved.

All of which reminds me of us. We all carry a name of which we are not quite worthy: Christian. I wonder how often we stop and think about the fact that we call ourselves after the name of the very Lord of heaven and earth, after Jesus the Christ. Talk about a name you have to live up to! If we carry that name heedless of its monumental power, we all too easily devalue it. Can we carry that name into sordid affairs and disreputable business without doing it and ourselves irreparable harm? Bearing the name Christian is like bearing the name "Grace": it carries with it tall expectations into which we have to grow. Given the life-changing beauty of the name, that's not such a bad thing.

The second thought that comes to mind, not surprisingly, is that we have to learn how to walk as Christians on our own. Many others can and will encourage us as we do so. They will be examples to us of what it means to live Christian lives, cheering for us when we do it well and comforting us when we stumble. For all that, though, no one else can be a Christian for us. Faithful as my father is and my mother was, neither can live my Christian life for me. I have to do it on my own, and doing it will mean taking my lumps along the way, eating my share of humble pie, stubbing my toe, and worse, all in order to figure out what it is that God has called me to be in Christ. In the long run, though, I know the joy to be reaped far outweighs the pain to be endured.

We all share this good name—Christian—and the high calling that goes with it. God has a purpose for each one of us, a calling that we alone can discover for ourselves by learning to walk in the way Christ would have us walk. Our first steps may be halting, but once we get the hang of it there will be no stopping us!

God bless us all as we toddle down the path of faith!

The Unexamined Life

Socrates said, "The unexamined life is not worth living." To appreciate fully the lives God has given us, truly to grow in directions we ought to grow, we need to look inside ourselves, to study our own motives, and to reflect on our basic orientations of life.

My experience as a home-owner and yard-maintainer, strangely enough, comes to mind in this context. You see, I make an effort to take good care of my yard. I mow it, trim it, fertilize it, and edge it. I spend some sweat on it and, in general, it looks pretty good.

But I completely neglect my flowerbeds. I suppose this goes back to the days when digging weeds was not a voluntary activity for my brothers and me, when, usually on the hottest day of a hot Dallas summer, my father would announce his intention that the garden be weeded.

"Fine, Dad," we'd sometimes joke. "Be sure to wear a hat out there. It gets awful hot."

"Wise guys get to weed the front and the back," he'd announce, and that would be the end of the discussion.

Since I never particularly enjoyed bending over all day, hot sun beating down on my head, breeze blocked by three surrounding walls, I never developed a "green thumb," or an appreciation for the threat to human order weeds represent. And it shows around my house, too.

Sometimes it bothers me that the only thing growing in the flowerbeds are rampant, hearty weeds. Sometimes I wish the beds looked better than they do. But unless and until I'm willing to invest a little sweat in pulling up the bad and pruning up the good, it just isn't going to happen.

What I see in my yard, I also see in my life. I've learned

that if I want the good things to grow in the "garden" of my life, I have to work at it. If I don't, the good things may grow, but I can rest assured that other things that aren't so good will also grow in abundance. It's anybody's guess as to which will prosper the most.

We discover what things are worth cultivating and what need weeding by the process of self-examination. In the act of listening to our hearts, of hearing the words of scripture, of reflecting on our experiences, we learn what matters, what builds up, and what tears down. Without self-examination, again, it's anybody's guess what we'll learn.

The unexamined life is a wild place. Yet its wildness is not the romanticized wildness of those who idolize nature. It is the wildness of a garden that produces nothing but weeds, of a life ruled by overmastering passions. In that wild place, we never say no to the desires that distort us, the greed that dehumanizes us, the selfishness that commands us. Do the good things stand a chance amidst this wildness? Ask the gardener.

To live well, we have to learn to look at ourselves and at others honestly. We must, in scripture's words, "Seek peace, and pursue it" (Psalm 34:14). We need to learn to value truth, even when it hurts; to practice justice, even to our personal disadvantage; and to cultivate prayer, even when the feeling of prayer is absent.

These things don't just happen. They require sweat in order to grow. As in the best of yards and gardens, the weeds will still be there, though under control. Yet in the end, this examined life, this cultivated garden of the heart, becomes an object of surpassing beauty, changing the lives of all who come in contact with it. It bears wonderful fruit, fruit well worth cultivating, the fruit of "love, joy, peace, patience, kindness, generosity, faithfulness, gentleness, and self-control" (Galatians 5:22–23).

Even to my lazy mind that's worth a little sweat.

Preventive Maintenance

Have you changed the oil in the car lately? I learned the hard way one time how important that kind of thing is. Still "wet behind the ears" after college, newly married, I was living in Chicago back in the pre–Jiffy Lube days. I distinctly remember the last thing my Dad said to me before Ann and I left Dallas for the frozen north: "Son, that car burns a little oil."

Well, I was busy. I was the assistant manager of a bookstore, working for a manager who was both drunk and "borrowing" from the till. They fired him just after I quit. Ann was working long hours at an architectural firm downtown. Seminary was still on the horizon. The hardest thing was that nagging question that kept running through my mind: "What's a native Texan doing in a place like this?"

To top things off, it was doggone cold! I realized a little bit of what was in store the first time I went to the outdoor mall in Oak Park and noticed that the bank sign gave the temperature as +73. Being the reflective sort, I reflected something along these lines: "Hmm, Johnny-boy, if that thing says *plus* 73 now, I bet it'll say *minus* something-or-other before I get out of here." Boy, was that ever right! I saw that darn sign once when it read -26! That's a long, long way from Rice University and Houston, Texas.

So, you might say preventive maintenance wasn't really at the top of my agenda. And one fine fall day as I was driving home down beautiful, tree-lined Oak Park Avenue, the car just up and died. No last words. No long, lingering departure. Do not pass go, do not collect $200, deader than the proverbial doornail on the spot. So take my word for it as someone who knows, it's cheaper to do a little preventive maintenance than to replace an engine! Have you changed that oil lately?

I guess that incident made quite an impression, because I've now gone into the preventive maintenance business myself. Obviously, I don't do much with cars. But in a sense, what we offer at church is preventive maintenance for our mental and spiritual health. We offer a way for people to check in with what is ultimately real, with God.

Carl Jung, the great psychologist, wrote about this. He said the healthiest people he knew, the ones who almost never came to him for treatment, were Catholics who regularly went to confession. Something in the process of being able to speak their deepest, darkest secrets before God and receive assurance of forgiveness gave these folks a balancing point in their lives. We Protestants sometimes joke about confession, but we really shouldn't.

Preventive spiritual maintenance keeps the soul running. Toxic secrets can burn up the engine when we can't let go of them. They become obsessions and we become closed off, suspicious people. But we don't have to be. If we check in with the God who loves us, totally unburden ourselves in God's presence, we control the secrets instead of vice-versa. Jung himself was agnostic, but what he called his "physician's heart" led him to encourage this very thing among his patients. Relating to God makes for mental health. We are spiritual beings.

So, bring that old soul in this Sunday for an oil change. Let God pop the hood and fiddle around inside. Let Jesus wash out the old oil, change the filter, and fill you up with the new oil of forgiveness and purpose.

Believe me, it's a lot cheaper to do the preventive maintenance now.

Recipe for Happiness

I am a notorious "experimenter" when it comes to cooking. If a recipe calls for such-and-so amount of a spice, I always wonder what happens if you double it. Unfortunately, my wife is often the victim of the experiments, and she has been known, on occasion, to let me know when the experiments fail.

There was the time, for instance, when I experimented with the red pepper in the chili recipe. Perhaps I should have known something was amiss when the chili fumes peeled the paint off the kitchen wall, or when the cat ran and hid when I offered him a sample. I didn't get the hint, though, until after Ann took the first bite.

When she began crying, I thought it must be because it was such wonderful chili. Those were tears of joy, I proudly thought to myself. They weren't. She hasn't let me near that recipe since. The chili was so hot it would probably still be good if we'd kept it in the refrigerator, but I think she called the toxic waste disposal team, and they came in their chemical suits and carted it off.

Oh well, if there's a lesson in everything, that bowl of chili certainly had its share. One was, "If the cat runs away from it, you should too." Another was, "Follow the recipe—that's what it's for." A third, perhaps, was, "When in doubt, eat out." Most important was the realization that, as with life in general, if you put too much of a certain thing into a recipe, you won't like what comes out.

All of which gets me to thinking about the things that go into the "recipe" of our lives. Three parts daily routine. Two parts stress. A tablespoon of humor and a dash of worry. So often the elements of the recipe are chosen haphazardly, and the results are at best mediocre. But we'll get out of it what we put into it, and if we're interested in getting something good out of it (and who isn't?), we need to take special care with the ingredients.

People who know best say the most effective seasonings in this recipe of life come from the faith group. A life seasoned with trust, stirred together with wonder, and baked with hefty portions of prayer tends to come out well. It has a strong flavor, tending toward the joyous. That is, after all, what Jesus' recipe calls for: "Seek first the kingdom of God and God's righteousness, and all else will be added to you..." (Matthew 6:33, author's translation).

Yet we get in such a hurry we forget to follow the recipe. Trust, wonder, and prayer are exotic enough ingredients that we haven't fully integrated them into our cooking style. When pressed for time, we revert to the old familiars: too often worry, anger, and frustration instead of faith, hope, and love. But hurried or not, we'll have to eat what we've put into the recipe.

That's what makes taking the time for faith so important in our lives. It builds good habits. It conditions us to give God the first thought, not the last. It reminds us on an ongoing basis that prayer is powerful and that our Lord can be trusted. It's like a cooking class for the soul. Taken regularly, it significantly increases our enjoyment of the life we "cook."

In the press of life, remember Christ's recipe, cook well, and enjoy. And by the way, if anybody gets hungry for chili, give me a call.

God bless you with good spiritual digestion!

When All We Can See Is Legs

It's tough when all you can see of the world around you is legs. Gracie, my one-year-old, and I were in the local Bookstop store over the holidays, doing our thing while Ann wrapped gifts up front. They built the store in an old theater, which makes it a toddler's paradise—long, sloping ramps from front to back, lots of stairs, plenty of railings to climb on. I'm not so sure the other patrons are as excited about it being a toddler's paradise as the toddlers themselves, but so be it. Kids will be kids.

Gracie and I were playing on the ramp. She'd run up it, look back at me, and I'd come after her while she shrieked with delight. She'd climb the railing like a little mountaineer, raising a tiny fist triumphantly when she got to the top. Then, if I didn't come get her down quickly enough, her triumph would turn to despair as she realized she couldn't get back down. (There's a sermon there on situations we can get ourselves into easily enough but can't get ourselves out of, but I'll save that for later.) All the while she was having a grand old time.

Then something happened that reminded me just how limited her view of the world is. We were playing the "run up the ramp while Dad chases me" game and I was still behind her. But while she was running, another man walked past me and then walked past her. Because all she could see was his legs, she thought it was me. At first, she was indignant that I would walk by and stop playing the game so abruptly. Then, indignation turned to fear. She thought for a moment she had been left alone in the middle of that big place, without a mom or a dad nearby. In the space of just a few seconds, the tears started to come.

In reality I hadn't left her at all. I was right behind her all the time, and before she could cut loose with the kind of cry that only abandoned toddlers can manage, I scooped her up in my arms and said, "It's all right, baby. Daddy hasn't left you alone." For an instant, her little face lit up with as much relief as I've ever seen. She gave me a big hug, then squirmed out of my arms and back into toddler wonderland.

It's tough when all you can see is legs. From that perspective, this world defies understanding. Things move faster than you can keep up with them. People speak a strange language you're only beginning to understand. So many things around you seem exciting, yet take away the ones who provide your security—even if only for a moment—and that excitement turns to terror. When all you can see of the world around you is legs, being alone is the worst nightmare.

You and I can see more than legs, fortunately, but I think we still can understand the toddler's perspective. We've learned to walk in this physical world, yet most of us are still toddling into that world of the spirit that is both the aim and reward of this physical life. We see it from a very limited perspective, and what we see of it is both tantalizing and terrifying at the same time. We need someone's sheltering presence, someone's constant love, to watch over us while we learn to make our way in this new dimension.

Yet because all we can see of this world is legs, we sometimes share that feeling of abandonment and desolation. We think the one who loves us has gone and left us alone. The fear paralyzes us, and we cry out in terror, even if those around us never hear us say a word. How can we look after ourselves when all we can see is legs? Simply put, we can't.

Yet that is the moment when the One who surrounds us with a parent's love comes to us and scoops us up into strong arms. In our terror, God speaks the word to us: "It's all right, my child. I haven't left you alone." And when we hear and believe that in the depths of our being, ah, what relief it is...even if all we can see is legs.

The Well

An ancient Chinese teacher once said to his disciples, "You can move the town anywhere you want, but you can't move the well." A village's life centered around the well in those days, a natural fact villagers ignored only at their peril. People drew their very lives from the well, gathered around it for social occasions, and saw it with a reverence bordering on awe most of the time.

Sometimes folks took the well for granted. They built their houses further and further into the fields, growing ever busier with their mundane concerns. In the midst of the bustle they forgot to tend the well. Its walls began to buckle and the spring feeding it slowly began to choke. Such calamity usually brought people's minds back to the essentials in short order. Neglect the well, after all, and there is no village, however sophisticated the villagers might think themselves.

The point, even twenty-five hundred years later, remains well taken. As individuals, we sometimes think we can live without the "well" in our lives. We push and push and push, pursuing every waking moment those things our hearts desire most. We lie in bed at night worrying about what we didn't get done and wake scheming about what we'll do next. There's nothing wrong with this, though sometimes it leaves us with a terrible thirst.

The same thing happens to us in our families. Husbands and wives get so busy they forget entirely what it was that first drew them together. Marriages wither like tender plants in the summer sun, for lack of water. This happens all the time in life, anytime people get too busy to enjoy their loved ones' company. Sometimes we get so far from the well we even forget there *is* a well, and that's a very thirsty way to live.

The point in all this is to remind us to stay close to the source! We fool ourselves if we think we can wander away from our well without drastic consequences to our own happiness and well-being, to say nothing of the welfare of those around us. And just where is our well? It bubbles up in a variety of places, actually.

It bubbles up preeminently in that place where we approach the God of Jesus Christ, in that interior oasis the Holy Spirit gives us through faith. Go there often enough and we will find sufficient refreshment to trust God and to live abundantly. There we taste the water of life that carries us beyond all cause for fear, washing away the stain of sin and the shadow of death. It so enriches our lives to drink from that well. I cannot help worrying about those who wander so far from it that they never even know it's there.

But that well also bubbles up in our personal and social lives, wherever we find that loving touch that refreshes us. I taste the well during my prayer time each morning, laughing at good jokes, and spending unhurried time with family and friends. I know where the well is, at least, even though I'm often a long way from it.

And I think we all know where the well is in our own lives. The problem is not so much knowing, but having the good sense to stay close enough to drink from it when we're thirsty. Move the town if you must, my friends in Christ, but never move it far from the source.

Spiritual Formation

In June of 1993, with a two-year-old in tow and (fortunately) a tank of gas, Ann and I drove into Monument Valley from southern Utah. Those of you who remember John Wayne's movies will most likely remember Monument Valley, since Wayne loved to film there. And, without a doubt, making that drive ranks in my memory as one of the most awe-inspiring, beautiful moments in my life.

The first thing that strikes you is simply the tremendous scale of things. We're used to inner-city life, where everything is right on top of everything else. Yet from the north end of Monument Valley a person can literally see two hundred miles on a clear day. Twenty to thirty-mile distances—trips that used to take all day for the Navajo who live there—seem a stone's throw off the roads. A human being just isn't a very big deal in a place like that.

The most striking features, obviously, are those marvelous stone formations looming like monstrous castles from the valley below. According to geologists, several hundred million years ago those formations were hidden under a mighty plateau. Yet drop by drop and eon by eon the region's infrequent rains weathered away the surrounding soil until only the rock endured. That the Navajos consider the present state of that process a holy place is not a surprise. Anyone who has ever driven through it will know immediately what they mean.

Thinking about those rock formations reminds me of another kind of formation that is very much on my mind these days. That is spiritual formation. It strikes me that the lives of our spirits are shaped much the same way the monuments of Monument Valley have been. We do not consciously set out and build a spiritual life, anymore than the Navajo built the monuments in the valley. But time and the process of living have a tendency to erode away all in us that is not founded on the rock.

We may begin life like that ancient plateau, with all around us seemingly equal. Yet we never stay that way. As time goes by, certain things give way around us and certain things remain firm. Certain dreams, ideas, and hopes prove false and fleeting. Others endure even the scouring of life's sorrows. Wisdom, for us, means learning how to tell the difference between the fleeting and the enduring.

You and I don't have hundreds of millions of years for the process to shape us, obviously. Fortunately, we don't need that much time. We have surrounding us the witness of those whose lives have been formed, those whose witness to what endures stands as eloquently as the monuments in Monument Valley. Life invites us, therefore, to follow in their footsteps and let the force that shaped them shape us.

Christian spiritual formation recognizes from its very beginning that, as the psalmists so often put it, "God is our rock." We know by faith that "Jesus Christ is the same yesterday and today and forever" (Hebrews 13:8). And what God through Christ has formed in our hearts will endure, even as the rest erodes away. The process is not painless by any means. But the end result is a life of surpassing, even breathtaking, beauty.

Attend to the One who endures. Let Christ's spirit erode away all that is not of him. Be molded, shaped, formed, into the image of "the Rock who is higher than I," into Jesus Christ himself. And know as you do so that sometimes the beauty I see in the lives of your spirits surpasses anything I saw at Monument Valley.

Making the Journey

I suppose I've wanted to see the northern lights, the aurora borealis, ever since I read the story about Nanak the Eskimo boy in my fourth-grade social studies class. Nanak would stand on a hillside at night, after a long day of seal hunting and other such "Eskimo" things, and raise his arms in harmony with the spectacular lights in the sky. I don't really remember what happened to him next. I suppose he went into his igloo and had Eskimo Pie for dinner. But for all the details I don't remember about the story, I remember the lights.

From all accounts, they are spectacular. "It's the most amazing thing you'll ever see," a friend of mine once said. "It's like the whole sky lights up with all the most brilliant colors of the rainbow! I've seen a lot of spectacular things in my life and been to lots of spectacular places, but I've never seen anything quite like that."

Sounds impressive, doesn't it! Someday I would love to see the lights. Maybe we can get a northern lights franchise to move to Houston so we can all see it together...but, then again, maybe not. I suppose for all the good things Houston has going for it, it's just too far south for the northern lights. We might not have to freeze to death in winter, but we won't see any outstanding light shows in the winter sky either, unless Astroworld happens to be open. And even that's not quite the same thing Nanak saw.

So, what is an aspiring northern lights viewer to do, who finds himself living in Houston? He can just forget about it, if it is not really that important. He can be satisfied with seeing pictures, reading stories about Nanak, and talking to old oil field hands from Alaska about it. But if he really wants to see them deep down in his soul, he has to make the trip because he'll never see them in Houston. If it's important enough that he wants to see it with his own eyes, there's just no other way.

All of which reminds me of the story from John's Gospel. Jesus is at a well and a Samaritan woman approaches. He, a Jew, asks for water. She, a Samaritan (Jews and Samaritans were the first-century equivalent of Aggies and Longhorns, Buckeyes and Wolverines, Bruins and Trojans, I guess), was shocked that he even spoke to her. Never having met her before, Jesus proceeded to tell her "everything she'd ever done."

She was beyond amazement at that point...probably even more amazed than I would be at seeing the lights. So she went back into her village and told her neighbors about Jesus. Some of them, no doubt, shrugged it off. Others said, "You tell me and that will be enough." But some could not be satisfied until they saw him for themselves. John records their words after they had seen Jesus: "It is no longer because of what you said that we believe, for we have heard for ourselves, and we know that this is truly the Savior of the world" (John 4:42).

If it's important enough to us to want to experience it for ourselves, we've got to make the journey. Whether it's seeing the northern lights or coming to know that One who is. If we want to know, we have to go. No one else can go for us. Yet the end of that journey will be spectacular beyond anything we've seen.

Pack the bags, honey, and put in sweaters and jackets. We have a trip to make.

Longing

One of my favorite hymns, "Above the Hills of Time," contains the following line, which has always intrigued me: "And for the love of Christ men's hearts are yearning/As shipwrecked seamen yearn for morning light." Our longing for God, the hymnwriter tells us, is as intense as the longing of those lost at sea for the light that brings them their salvation. Is it really? If we listed the things we yearn for, would the love of Christ top the list? On the most obvious level the answer would have to be no. As proof, ask yourself what you desire most, what you long for, right now. Are you longing for dinner, perhaps? Is your mind fixated on an upcoming vacation (I know mine is!)? Do you want that job, that promotion, that new car or house more than anything else in the world? Of all the things we long for, does God's love even make the list? In an overt way, probably not.

And yet on a deeper level, who knows? The most enlightening course I took in seminary was pastoral counseling, during which we served as our own guinea pigs. Perhaps the most important lesson I learned from those three intense months of introspection had to do with understanding my own desires for what they actually are on that deeper level.

On the surface, for example, the longing is for vacation—to get out of the office, have a change of pace, relax, and renew. Yet the deeper dimensions of that longing include an inner insecurity, a desire for fulfillment, and a realization that, at times at least, work can't provide those things. What is that emptiness inside that leads me to long for a vacation this time of year, and what can fill it? Well, I know in advance that the vacation doesn't cure the emptiness, and that when I get back, I'll long for something else just as superficially. As a matter of fact, my garage is full of past "longings" that material acquisitions didn't quite meet—a bicycle, a weight set, an electric guitar, and so forth.

What do we long for on that deeper level? What can fill that gnawing, unnamable emptiness inside? Advertisers are masters of manipulating us into thinking new experiences, new gadgets, and new possessions can do it, but can they? On honest reflection, we realize that, despite Madison Avenue's constant preachments, they simply can't.

What we long for at the deepest level is security, affirmation, meaning, peace. In a world as filled with uncertainty as our own, surrounded as we are by our own mortality and that of all those we love, we long for the certainty that our lives matter. We long for the good news, spoken to our spirits and not just our minds, that who we are and what we are is secure in this insecure world. This may sound unlikely because we are conditioned to label that longing differently, but examine your heart and you'll find it's true.

And, friends, that longing can only be met at the level of spirit. That emptiness can only be filled in relationship to One who is not limited, not threatened, not finite. I believe such a One exists, the One we call God, and the most compelling demonstration of God's power is precisely the love of Christ that conquers death.

I also believe that the day will come in every life when the blinders are taken off and we will see the true source of our emptiness. In that seeing we will realize the futility of trying to fill it with possessions. And we will also see the eternal willingness of God, through that very love of Christ, to fill what is lacking in our hearts.

Do we long for Christ's love "as shipwrecked seamen yearn for morning light"? You bet we do. All praise to the One who can answer that longing.

Near to the Heart of God

"There is a place of quiet rest," the old hymn says, "near to the heart of God." And there is also such a place within us.

By quieting ourselves and looking inside, by letting go, if only for a moment, of the desires to do, to get, and to have, which drive us so relentlessly, we discover to our amazement that this place of peace exists.

And discovering, we go there to rest. The troubling thoughts that so often molest arise, yet while we are there we simply let them go. Desires erupt, yet in that place the urgency to fulfill them is strangely lacking. There we rest and are renewed.

Who knows whether this quiet, unhurried place within us is not in fact very "near to the heart of God"? Who knows whether we are so deeply imbedded in the One "in whom we live and move and have our being," as Paul put it in Acts, that to be deeply within our hearts is to be in God's heart also? The only way to answer the question is to visit the place and see for ourselves.

Forget about the world outside for a moment—it will still be there when you get through. In this relaxed state, imagine that the love of God shines in your heart, a solitary beam of beautiful light. Imagine that light filling you on the inside, illuminating every dark corner and crevice with its beam of love. Imagine, further, that the same light that fills you, fills every person around you today, every person in your hometown, in your state, in your nation, in your world.

In your imagining, know that this beautiful light is always present, always faithful, always loving, always ready to fill you with peace. It never moves, never flickers, never fades, however seldom we look for it. Imagine this, and remember that Jesus said, "I am the light of the world" (John 8:12).

Those who know about such things tell us that when we practice being "near to the heart of God," we find ourselves changing. Go to that place often enough, and that place becomes a present reality, even in the midst of life's turmoil. Go to that place often enough, see in it the light of God's love filling not only us but all that lives, and others cease being our enemies. In the light of God's love, we begin to see those around us as children of God and children of light.

Go to that quiet place often enough, and the peace God gives us there begins to well up in our hearts and spill over into our world.

The wise women and men of old, those whose love for others made a difference, called this the "practice of the presence of God." For them, life held no greater reward, offered no greater joy. May we follow in their footsteps.

A Mysterious Beginnings

According to cosmologists, those scientists who study the origins of the universe, everything began at a moment called "Planck Time," so called after Max Planck, the "father" of quantum physics. In case you wonder, "Planck Time" looks like this:

.0000000000000000000000000000000000000000001 seconds.

All subsequent time dates from that instant. To talk about time "before" that instant is absurd, because there was nothing for which time existed.

The universe expanded more in the first instant of its existence than it has in all the estimated 15 billion years that have followed. Furthermore, what we can see of the universe is a tiny one percent of the whole. Ninety-nine percent of it remains hidden from us, so-called "dark matter," the existence of which can only be inferred mathematically.

Prior to the explosion the cosmologists call the "Big Bang," everything that now constitutes this universe was compressed into an almost inconceivably small, unfathomable hot point, much smaller than an atom. Everything that was, is, and will be, past, present, and future, all jammed into an indescribable something (Someone?) that by the very limitations of our minds must remain a mystery to us. No human mind by its own light can penetrate to the reason behind the explosion.

This event has been unfolding ever since, and we are a part of it. Its energy is that which gives us life. Its destiny is our destiny. Its mystery is our mystery. We are, the cosmologists might say, children of this ongoing, universal event. We are not separate from it. There is no objectivity outside it. To borrow the words of an ancient theologian, it is that "in which we live and move and have our being." Different as all of us may be, we have a fundamental unity in this universal event that transcends all our differences.

What strikes me about this description of the beginning is how remarkably similar it is to the Judeo-Christian creation story in Genesis 1:1–2:4. The original Hebrew describes an ongoing event, too, a gradual unfolding of all that is from its original, unfathomable source. The verse translated as "In the beginning...God created the heavens and the earth" can just as accurately be rendered, "From the beginning God has been creating the heavens and the earth."

Cosmologists today use the language of mathematics and physics to describe that which the mystics and visionaries of old described in the language of poetry and story. There's no doubt in my mind they are describing the same reality. And it's worth reviewing what the various versions of the story have in common:

- The universe is a mystery that awes and captivates us;
- We are a part of and one with an unfolding process, the end of which is also mysterious;
- Our lives are unique and valuable events within this process;
- The One from whom all things come defies all our descriptions, and yet is the source of all that was, is, and will be.

Our name for this mysterious One is God. I hope that we will learn to treasure all insights into the nature of that wondrous One, whatever name is applied.

In the year ahead, may we wonder at this marvelous mystery we call life, love those with whom we share it, and honor the One who has given it to us!

May Christ's peace fill all of us.

The God to Whom We Pray

All too often, our theology is the major obstacle to a genuine life of prayer. For some reason, many of us never grow beyond a "Man Upstairs" image of God—God as an old man with a white beard sitting on a throne somewhere above us, pulling all the strings in a puppet world below.

That theology permeates much of what passes for prayer in our world today. You hear it expressed when the coach tells the media after the tournament that "God gave us the victory," as if this beneficent ruler had intentionally given all the other teams defeat. Any time prayer is selfish, any time it aims solely for the benefit of an individual or group, rest assured the "Man Upstairs" is being addressed.

The problem with this sort of prayer is that the theology behind it is flawed, as we realize when we face tragedy and hardship in our lives. Such moments teach us that if God is a puppeteer, God is a cruel one at that. In such circumstances we can't explain why the God we once thought guided us to victory now makes us suffer. Such questions can lead us to conclude there is no God or that, if there is, such a God isn't worth wasting prayer on. And since prayer is the cornerstone of Christian living, it's a small step from that decision to the decision to have nothing to do with the church or other Christians.

God is not at fault here, however. The difficulty arises because the "Man Upstairs" image is not an adequate understanding of our Creator. God and Santa Claus aren't one and the same. To taste the kind of prayer that can be a cornerstone for effective living, our understanding both of God and of prayer needs to grow.

Prayer is more than talking to God. Prayer is communion with and openness to God. Such prayer assumes not that God is some distant "Man Upstairs" who has to be talked into doing what we want, but that God is with us, indeed that God is in us. Jesus said as much: "The kingdom of God is within you" (Luke 17:21). Paul quoted the Greek philosophers to make the same point during his sermon in Athens: "[God] is not far from each one of us, for 'in him we live and move and have our being'" (Acts 17:27–28).

We would do better addressing our prayers to this One who is closer to us than we are to ourselves, this One who in the words of Genesis "breathes into our nostrils the breath of life." Prayer that operates under this theology can be powerful. Through such prayer, we find a continued awareness of God's presence, perhaps through repeating verses of scripture again and again or by imagining God's presence as a point of light within us.

Through such prayer, we understand that God is never absent from our lives, that our lives would be unimaginable apart from God. Further, we understand through it God's presence in every living being, and we seek to live respectfully in light of it. Such prayer does not grant us an exemption from suffering, yet it does offer us a communion with God that gives us strength to face that suffering. "I can do all things," Paul said, "through [Christ] who strengthens me" (Philippians 4:13).

With such prayer we know that God is not a "Man Upstairs" to be met "in the sky, by and by." God is here and eternally now, the One in whom past, present, and future all exist, the One whose presence is its own reward. Such prayer harnesses all the gifts God gives—intellect, imagination, action, and emotion—to that communion that inspires our love for others and provides "peace that surpasses all understanding."

That sounds like something worth pursuing.

Scripture's First Theologian

She is scripture's first theologian. Hagar, maidservant to Sarai, wife of Abram, was an Egyptian slave. When we meet her in scripture, the family to which she is in bondage is in crisis. Abram, its head, is growing old. Rich as he is, he has no heir and this troubles him greatly. Sarai, Abram's wife, is also growing older, feeling quite threateningly not only the "ticking of her biological clock" but also the scorn of her society toward women who could not bear children.

Sarai solves her problem in a manner common to the society of her day. She "gives" her maidservant Hagar to Abram to bear a child that in the eyes of the law and society will officially be considered Sarai's. The well-to-do often resorted to this practice in such situations. What Hagar's thoughts were on the subject we can only imagine. No one in Abram's household would have bothered about her thoughts anyway.

The deed was done and Hagar became pregnant with Abram's child. Far from being pleased by this, Sarai turned against Hagar and made her life increasingly miserable. In desperation, the pregnant Hagar ran away into the wilderness where, undoubtedly thirsty and scared, she had a vision of the Lord.

In her awed response, she called this being "the God who sees me," capturing in that brief title the wonder of a Lord who was concerned even for the welfare of a homeless slave woman. For the first time in scripture, a human being pauses to describe God, explicitly to "do theology" (theology from the Greek *theos*, "God," and *logos*, "talk"). Hagar talks about, thinks about, and ultimately marvels at the grace of the God who sees. Others before her had responded to God without deliberation, but none had "done theology" the way Hagar did it there in the wilderness. Hagar, therefore, is the first theologian, and every human being who cares enough about faith to think about and talk about God is her spiritual descendent.

We as Christians share Hagar's vocation, having been called by Paul to "work out our salvation with fear and trembling." I've read a lot of theology in my life, and I know that the best kind is the kind that arises out of the actual experience of God's presence in our lives. This theology begins when we, like Hagar, come to know God intimately.

What does our experience tell us God is like? Unfortunately, most of us have never known God well enough to give God a name. Our words come from other people's experiences, rather than our own. This lack of personal experience makes our religious lives at best irrelevant and at worst narrow and hateful. When we mistake words about God with God's actual self, we often take great offense at those who name God differently. "Religious" wars are fought by persons who have never come close enough to God to know that no genuine disciple could ever make war in God's name.

Our faith, therefore, invites us to join Hagar in drawing so close to God that our name for God arises out of our own experience. Such names always seem similar: not "God whom we fear," or "Pitiless Judge," but "Compassionate One," "God of Hope," "Author of Peace." To experience God intimately is to know that God is love and that God's purpose in human affairs is reconciliation. All other "gods" are idols.

May all of us come to know the "God who sees" even us.

NO PUPPET LOVE

Puppets are a lot of fun, aren't they? You can make them say anything you want, they never wantonly disobey, and they'll love you without reservation and not be shy about saying so in public. There is no limit to how you can shape your puppet...other than the limit imposed by the puppet's utter inability to choose for itself. Think what a world we could create if we could fill it with puppets, as long as the right person was the puppeteer. No doubt we would be the right person, if only we had the chance.

The idea is so compelling, one wonders why God didn't think of it to begin with. Look at the world we now inhabit, with all its terrible problems. Some people feast while others starve. Some laugh while others weep. Some hate while others struggle to love. If we are puppets, God must be a lousy or even a downright malicious puppeteer.

We aren't puppets, though. In fact we are so completely independent of outside manipulation, so much "anti-puppets," that we can barely control ourselves, much less allow anyone else to control us. And, from a certain perspective, that's too bad.

If we were puppets, the puppeteer could cause us to act generously, be civil to one another, even attend to the needs of the puppets around us. Heck, I bet the puppeteer could even make us behave more reasonably in traffic. No more of this driving 50 mph in the fast lane on US 59.

Alas, though, we aren't puppets. As I said, from a certain perspective that's too bad. I am not a person without vices, minor though they may be. Yet minor or not, I have often wished there were a great puppeteer who could remove them from me. Why have such a temper? Why be unable to sit peacefully in traffic? How often have I prayed, "O God, give me patience...and give it to me **RIGHT NOW**!"

But we're not puppets. Our bad habits are just that—ours. No one's going to magically remove them. People will continue to feast while others starve. They will keep on putt-putting down the freeway, holding up those of us rushing to attend to important matters. They will keep being people, for gosh sakes. And is that really too bad?

It is if we want to live in a perfect world, a world without pain. Yet at this point, I suppose we at least need to consider the wisdom of the Creator. God being God, I'm sure the Creator could have made us without faults. We could have been "hard-wired" to do the right thing, to make the humane choice, in all circumstances. And, face it, driving would be much more civilized in such a world.

But what would be lost? Only our freedom to choose. There's a wonderful scene from the movie *A Clockwork Orange*, in which a young British delinquent has been psychologically conditioned to become physically ill if he contemplates an act of violence. It isn't that he wants to be a good citizen; he simply has no choice. The only person who objects to this is a clergyman who stands and shouts in an outraged voice, "You've rendered him incapable of making a moral decision!" Never mind that all his moral decisions had heretofore been immoral. Remove the capacity to make them and you have made a puppet, not a human being.

And for some reason God wanted human beings, not puppets. Do you suppose it's that God never had to drive in Houston traffic? Or could it be that God wants something more from us and for us than puppet-love? We'd live in a problem-free world without our freedom to choose, no doubt, but where in that world would we find genuine love?

Maybe that's what matters most after all.

God's Power

Power is interesting, isn't it? Most of us think of power as the ability to compel something or someone to do what we want. Power equals force, in other words. Those who possess such power are free and those who don't are helpless without it.

For the most part, that's how power works in human affairs, and since that's how it works with us, we assume that's how it works with God. God's power has always been conceived as human power writ large—all the great religious traditions are full of images of God as divine king, the eternal tyrant whose will cannot be questioned or understood.

Of course, it is hard to call such a God "good," if we're honest with ourselves. If this all-compelling God orders everything, how can we explain undeserved suffering? How do we justify God's goodness in the face of natural calamities, freak accidents, or war? While we may think that some folks "deserve" what they're getting through such tragedies, certainly not all of them do. What about the innocent, the children?

Is such an arbitrary God "good"? Hardly. And since this is the prevailing view of God's power in our world, it isn't surprising so many of us reject God. Not many of us profess to be atheists, of course, perhaps out of fear of God's arbitrary power. But more of us than we care to admit are "practical atheists," nominal believers who live our lives without reference to God. Why bother, we think, since it seems to make so little difference?

Yet there are other ways of understanding God's power. There is another kind of power in our world, a power that sets people free rather than taking their freedom away. This is the power of persuasion, the power that opens our eyes to new possibilities. This sort of power does not compel others and does not make its way by force. Instead, it gently coaxes, draws, and invites us to higher ways of living and seeing.

An example may prove helpful. If we see others in this world as our enemies (either personally or nationally), the first type of power deals with that by attempting to compel them to do our will. Since this often proves impossible, the exercise of such power in this world almost always involves compromise and has its winners and losers.

The second type of power, however, works not by compulsion but by persuasion. If you and I consider ourselves enemies, then this new type of power works to open our eyes to a new way of seeing each other. If you are my enemy and I hate you for it, I probably don't even see you as human. Yet, if I begin to see you, my enemy, as a human being with human needs and human pains very much like my own, my hatred is diminished. And if, through the power of persuasion, I come to see you as God's creation, eternally beloved, then even if I don't agree with your actions, I cannot help loving you.

What changes under the second scenario is not the external situation, so much, as the heart of the one involved in it. The power that enables me to see my "enemy" in a new light gives me a freedom I would never have had under the old way of seeing—the freedom to forgive, to understand, to change.

To my mind, that's the kind of power God exercises in this world—not the power to compel but the power to persuade. Jesus said, "And I, if I am lifted up, will draw all people to myself" (John 12:32). Notice he doesn't say "force," but rather "draw." That's the way love works. And if God's power works this way, perhaps we should change the way we exercise human power, so that it may work gently, too. When power works this way, the only thing that suffers is hatred.

May God love us all into a new way of seeing.

A Child's Love

It's wonderful being loved, isn't it? Since my daughter's birth, it's occurred to me that the biblical image of God's love being like a parent's love for a child perhaps gets things a little backward. Unconditional love is the love of a child for a parent—at least the love of a young child. The parent, in the child's eyes, can do no wrong, is the source of all comfort, and provides all security. Those are high expectations, of course, yet parents discover the power the child's love possesses. It changes us. It teaches us what unconditional love is all about.

I have to confess that nothing enrages me quite the way reports of child abuse do. It gets to the point sometimes where I have to turn off the television during the news because I just can't stand to watch it. When we parents lose control and take it out on our children, what words can be said in our defense? What can be said to those who violate that most basic trust, who scorn that unconditional love?

Yet, as those who know will tell us, the children continue to love the parents. They love them in spite of the abuse. They love them, arms outstretched, eyes teary, minds uncomprehending. They love them because it is their nature to love. If Paul's statement in 1 Corinthians 13 that "love never ends" ever needed proof, there is the proof.

Perhaps the children sense intuitively the pain, the confusion, the ignorance in their parents' hearts. Perhaps in the race between unconditional love and uncomprehending rage, love will win. Maybe the children's love will convert the parents to a new way of living before the parents' anger converts the children. Perhaps. What is certain is that the cost of either conversion is suffering—innocent, undeserved suffering.

We approach Palm Sunday with the image of a child's love in our minds. The child is God. The bearer of the child's love is Jesus of Nazareth. He comes to his people bearing a message that sets so many of them free. In his love so many find healing for body and spirit, comfort for mind and heart, and hope for the soul. His love, like a child's love, changes those around him.

And yet the abuser waits within the hearts of the people, also. The abuser waits, the one who cannot accept unconditional love and damns those who dare to love "inappropriately." What ensues is a race, of sorts: will Christ's child-like love convert God's people before they turn on him and kill him?

We call it Palm Sunday, this day when we remember Jesus' final entry into Jerusalem. They greeted him with branches cut from trees, with shouts of celebration, with joy, much the way we greet newborn children. And before the week ended, they killed him on a cross. Love lost the race; hatred won.

Yet did it? It's always tempting to leap to the story's end, to celebrate Easter's resurrection prematurely, but Holy Week comes one aching day at a time. We have to experience the ache of love betrayed before we can truly appreciate the joy of love triumphant.

God loves us the way a child loves a parent. Yet the abuser lurks in our hearts, too. We point fingers at others and find those fingers pointing back at us. This week we wonder, who will win the race between love and hatred in our hearts?

Our hope, our redemption, remains this: this childlike love of God is unconditional. It longs for us, arms outstretched, eyes teary, love undaunted.

Perhaps this week our hearts will be converted.

Moon Festival

The Japanese celebrate a festival each year in honor of the moon. One evening a year, when the moon is full and the sky (hopefully) is clear, people get together outside, have dinner, and share conversation, the moon being the point of the evening. The only restrictions are: (1) one may not say the word "moon," and (2) one may not point at the object in the sky. This is probably great fun for the children, who delight in the absurdity of it, and it's an opportunity for adults to enjoy each other's company, too.

Yet there's a meaning beyond the absurdity of the festival. The Japanese are sophisticated people and don't worship the moon. Yet the moon has great symbolic value in their faith traditions. The moon symbolizes the ultimate, God. It also symbolizes that place within ourselves where God's life flows into ours, where we are one with our Creator. Clouds, of course, can obscure the moon, making the festival somewhat problematic at times. But more serious are those "inner clouds" that can obscure what the moon symbolizes inside us, and much religious practice is devoted to dispelling them.

So, why be careful not to say "moon" or point at it during the festival? The theory goes that as soon as the word is spoken, it has become the object of the festival, rather than the real moon in the sky. As soon as we point, too, the pointing finger and not the moon has become the object of attention. The paradox is striking: to make the moon itself the focus of the festival, great care is taken not to mention it or point to it. We allow it to make its own statement by being what and where it is, and silence our own hearts so as to hear it.

Ponder the connection to matters of faith. While instruction about God is necessary, there is a point beyond which it can also become dangerous. In saying the word "God" with our own peculiar emphases so often and so long, we can get to the point where we make the word itself the focus of our faith, rather than the reality behind it. We make our particular manner of pointing at God more important than God. So, from time to time, it seems like a good idea to keep a "Moon Festival" of our own, if only to remind ourselves to be humble about the words we use for God. In keeping this "Moon Festival" of our spirits, we will resolve to allow God to be God and also resolve ourselves to listen.

Come to think of it, that sort of "festival" would be a great idea for Holy Saturday, with Christ's crucifixion behind us and his resurrection in front of us. Let's wait, hold our tongues, and see what God's Spirit has to say to us.

My prayer for all of us this Easter is that we will learn to celebrate the vast variety of ways our fellow human beings have of seeing the "moon." May we learn from them and rejoice with them, even as we share with them the supreme joy we have found in the love of Jesus Christ. The way of life he embodies may be called different names by different peoples, but it remains his way. Let us honor all who walk that way in sincerity.

Incidentally, I hope you enjoyed that big yellow thing up in the night sky. It was full last week.

Taste God

Ever tried to describe a taste? A friend of mine exposed me to Lebanese food shortly after I came back to Houston in '92. I'd never had it before, but I'm usually willing to try anything once, so off we all went to Sammy's Restaurant on the west side. The friend didn't waste his time trying to describe it to me. I had to taste it. There was no other way.

I think the same thing works in the life of faith, the difference being that too many of us haven't realized it yet. We are the inheritors of a tradition that has spent a tremendous amount of energy trying to describe the indescribable. We Christians have hashed and rehashed the theological essentials of our faith for nearly two millennia now, even fought wars over minor differences in the descriptions. But it wasn't always that way.

In the beginning, "Christianity" was just a dozen or so intimate friends gathered around a man named Jesus. They ate with him, studied with him, wandered with him. So far as we can tell, none had any "gainful" employment. All depended on the charity of strangers. In fact, we might have harsh words for people like that today.

But these intimate friends absorbed through their very pores the essence of what Jesus' life and faith were all about. They came to pray as he prayed, love as he loved, seek as he sought. Each Gospel makes clear they made mistakes on the way. They stumbled and fell. But part of the experience of being with Jesus was realizing that he loved them in spite of it. And, they came to realize, if he loved them, God loved them. Those disciples soon lost the ability to say where Jesus ended and God began. The two were obviously one, in a way they could neither explain nor deny.

The realization that Jesus and God were one led to the realization that God and the disciples were one. In the most down-to-earth sense we can imagine, those crusty fisher-folks experienced the rush of freedom that comes when heavy burdens are lifted. Seeing Jesus overcome death, they felt to the core of their beings their own deaths had been overcome also. It's like putting down heavy suitcases you've had to lug past your normal endurance, only infinitely more intense. Utter relief! Utter freedom! A completely new beginning!

After they experienced this, they described it to others, and others came to share the experience also. The inner truth was transmitted across generations. Somewhere along the line, though, we became willing to substitute words *about* faith for the personal experience *of* faith. We stopped tasting and started arguing.

The good news is this taste is still available to us. God lives in our midst just as powerfully today as he did twenty centuries ago. Human hearts are still as capable of receiving revelation now as they were then. The only thing lacking is the willingness to seek that taste with our whole hearts.

I've really taken a liking to Lebanese food in the last four years, which makes me glad I went and tasted for myself instead of settling for a description. Let's do that with faith, too.

The Tornado of God's Spirit

Even by the low standards of television news reporting, this was a dumb question. A Dallas TV reporter standing in the storm-ruined wreckage of a man's home said, "When did you notice something was different?" In shock as he was, even the homeowner couldn't abide that one. With smirking understatement, he answered, "When the storm blew the roof off the house, I knew I had a problem."

Some things aren't subtle. Rather than creeping up on us, they prefer instead to blow through our lives like tornadoes, leaving debris in their wake. Many of the various crises of health and employment come on us that way, as do midlife crises. In fact, it seems that most of life's sudden occurrences are bad, like the tornado or the heart attack.

In reality, though, they aren't. Pentecost Sunday recounts the most positive windstorm that has ever struck the human race. Pentecost was one of the ancient pilgrim festivals in Judaism, when good Jews from around the world made their way to Jerusalem to worship God. Rooted in Israel's agrarian rhythms, the festival marked the beginning of summer. The crops had been planted, the fields prepared, and Israel gathered during the time of waiting and hoping.

Yet for one group on Pentecost Sunday nearly two millennia ago, there wasn't much hoping going on amidst the waiting. These Galileans had remained in Jerusalem following the execution of their leader because they didn't have anything else to do. They had left behind lives and livelihoods to follow Jesus and had nothing to go back to. There is never a "back to" for people who know Jesus so intimately. Those disciples knew Jesus had been resurrected, but they still weren't sure what that meant for them.

In that upper room on Pentecost they found out. As they worshiped together, the room shook, as if rocked by a mighty wind. They felt welling up inside them a mighty conviction that this resurrected one was the Lord and Savior of the world. God moved among them like a tornado, blowing the roofs off their houses of despair, denial, and doubt. Those trembling disciples went forth that day to proclaim to the world a truth that the day before they had been afraid to even speak! "When did you notice something was different?" Perhaps at the moment when the world turned upside down.

I can see why the Greek word for "spirit" also has the meaning of "wind." Sometimes God's presence among us is a gentle zephyr, cooling God's people's heated brows. Sometimes it's a tornado, blowing away our apathy and transforming us into people on fire for their Lord. The mode of the Spirit's appearance depends entirely upon what we genuinely need (not necessarily what we want!) to get us going.

As we celebrate Pentecost, the birthday of Christ's church on earth, I pray that the tornado of God's Spirit will blast through our lives. May we latter-day disciples reach the point where we come alive for Christ, just like those first-century disciples before us! This moment can't be rushed; it doesn't come without waiting, seeking, and praying. But when in God's good time it does come, nothing is ever the same!

"When did you notice that something was different?" Our transformed lives will let God's glory speak for itself.

Genuine Freedom

Some things are designed to set us free. Some things are designed to help us stay free. In the biblical story, it is clear that God's grace toward us, God's unmerited favor, is the source of our freedom. When we respond in faith and trust, God frees us from sin, from the debilitating scars of the past, from apathy, from meaninglessness.

God does this for a purpose: As Paul says, we receive both "grace and apostleship" (Romans 1:5). Grace, as wondrous as it is, is not the last word. Apostleship is part of the bargain. The Greek word *apostello* means "to send." We are sent, compelled even, by the grace of God to share the good news with the world.

Good news takes different forms in different places. For a prisoner torn with guilt, good news is God's forgiving love even for the greatest sinners among us. For starving children in refugee camps, good news is a warm meal, medical care, hope for the future. For prosperous folks like us, good news is the opportunity to commune with Christ and share his work throughout the world. Having received grace, though, we accept the apostleship, the commissioning to share the good news, that comes with it.

How do we maintain the freedom God bought for us? God answered that question after delivering Israel from slavery in Egypt by giving them the Ten Commandments. You can read the actual text of the commandments in two places, Exodus 20:1–17 and Deuteronomy 5:1–21. I have paraphrased them below for your reflection.

1. Be reverent of the whole.

2. Worship God, not the work of your hands.

3. Be aware of the power of your words.
4. Take time to listen, especially to God.
5. Treat family members with respect, regardless of their age.
6. Treasure life—yours and others'.
7. Respect promises and those to whom you make them.
8. Respect property.
9. Be truthful.
10. Remember that your life is God's creation, too.

Jesus summed it up better than anyone else can. "Do to others what you would have them do to you" (Matthew 7:12, alt.).

That's the recipe for keeping our freedom.

Power for Christian Living

I had an interesting experience recently. Life, as it tends to for ministers around Easter, had gone crazy. I had three thousand things to do, good things for the most part, yet it's funny how even "good" things can become more of a burden than we either want or can stand sometimes.

When that happens, I take on the characteristics of a grouchy old bear. But something happened in the midst of doing the three thousand things on my list. At least one of those things involved picking up my Bible, doing some study preparation, and spending some time in prayer. In the course of notching those things off my "to do" list, I was, in C. S. Lewis' words, "surprised by joy." Spending time in the presence of God had been just another "thing" to do. But in the act of doing it, God's spirit was there with the kiss of joy.

Joy is like that, I've discovered. It pops up in the most unlikely circumstances sometimes. It seems highly unlikely to me that I would encounter something so sublime when I'm in my "grouchy bear" mode. It just doesn't seem like I have time for it. But there it was, unexpected yet certainly not unwelcome, like a surprise visit from a cherished old friend.

On the other hand, it really shouldn't be all that surprising that we encounter joy in the midst of our days. After all, joy is the fruit of human contact with the love of God and we are, whether we are aware of it or not, surrounded by that love. We may not be in happy circumstances all of the time, but happiness and joy aren't the same thing. Even in unhappy times joy can still surface, and so it often does.

Sometimes, in my mad dash to get through everything on my list, I forget the power inherent in Christian living. Don't get me wrong. I don't pretend it's my power. Nevertheless, ministry has taught me again and again that in basic "church things," in Bible study and worship, in prayer and singing, in service and action, there is power. These things may be part of my routine, but they are never "routine" themselves.

In fact, sometimes I feel like the light company employee who pushes the buttons down at the power plant. In the humdrum of daily life he may forget just what power courses through those buttons. It isn't his, of course; nevertheless, when he pushes the right buttons, the whole city lights up. And when he doesn't, things are strangely dark.

God's power is present in the routine things we do in the church. It's not our power, by any stretch. But when we pray, worship, study, and serve, God's power is unleashed through us and beyond us many times, whether we're aware of it or not. Those moments when we become aware of it oftentimes overwhelm us with the joy of the love of God.

I think it's safe to say that many who criticize the church do so only from a safe distance. If they were to come too close and get "zapped" by the love of God, they'd find they couldn't be critics any longer. And that's a good reason for us to make church routine part of our routine.

So, friends, let me offer a word of warning about coming to church. It may seem routine to you. You may get up, shower, dress, and leave the same way you always do (either every Sunday or at least this one Sunday a year). True, you may be a little more tired than usual if you come to the sunrise service, and it may be a little harder to park than usual at the main service. But much of the day may seem routine.

Don't let looks deceive you, though. This routine isn't "routine." There will be power in our worship service Sunday. Oh, don't misunderstand me. It won't be our power. But it will be there, all the same. And in the process of "pushing the buttons," of singing hymns, hearing scripture, and partaking of sacraments, don't be surprised if you are surprised, even overwhelmed, by joy! That's what the power of God does when it comes into our hearts, whether we're ready or not.

Deeper Layers of Spirit

Warning: not for the claustrophobic!!!!

I learned something interesting about the submarine business not long ago. There's something called the thermal layer in the ocean, where the deep ocean's cold water comes in contact with the warmer waters near the surface. Above that layer, the water is turbulent, swept by all the currents from the surface and heated by the sun's warmth. Below it, things become very still and quiet.

This is significant in the submarine business. Above the layer, a submarine is subject to all the turbulence from the currents and winds. Since warmer water carries sound more readily, the sub is also extremely vulnerable to sonar. It sails naked when it's close to the surface, something submariners don't necessarily favor.

Below the layer, things change dramatically. The colder water reflects the sonar back, so the sub is virtually invisible from the surface. The ride becomes much smoother, since the cold water doesn't move around as much. Those who've been to that depth describe it as being amazingly tranquil, serene, and secure. The mechanism of getting there is also interesting. A sub can only go deep by blowing out its excess air. If it keeps all that inside, it can only stay on the surface. But once it's blown off its steam, so to speak, it can go as deep as its own structure will allow.

This offers predictable advantages. Old Navy salts say no ride is rougher than that of a submarine on the surface. The shape of its hull magnifies every wave so that, in any type of rough weather, the sub will bounce around like a nervous colt. Even hard-bitten sailors are known to get seasick under such circumstances.

Then, there's the problem of detection. The closer a sub is to the surface, the more dangerous its predicament. It relies on stealth, on depth, on surprise, and it loses those very elements when it's "above the layer." But when it dives deep, it has a lot more room and time to deal with problems. It can steam around contacts if it needs to, or bide its time and evaluate situations without having to take immediate action. It can run away safely if circumstances dictate, or attack with all its advantages in play if that's what is needed. The depth, though, is what provides the luxury of deliberation. Above the layer there is no such luxury

. All of which reminds me a great deal of life. There's a "thermal layer" inside us, too. Above that layer, near the surface, we face endless storms and crises, a turbulent world without end. We bounce around like a sub on the surface, far more vulnerable than we'd like to be. Granted, all of us have to spend some time "above the layer." Unfortunately, most of us spend far more time there than we have to, to our own harm.

But there's a deeper layer in life, the layer of God's Spirit within us. Once we plunge to that depth, we too find an immense, peaceful calm, a place from which we can make solid, unhurried decisions. In that place, we have the luxury of being able to decide which contact to back away from, which to wait out, and which to confront head on. We don't have to fight each fight down there. We get to pick and choose.

We live the Christian life most effectively when we take time to dive "below the layer," deep into the ocean of God's presence. It renews us by easing our minds. And it empowers us to come to the surface again with a fresh sense of who we are, whose we are, and what we are here to do.

Dive deep, friends in Christ, now and always!

Lies, Lies, Lies

It hit me one Saturday recently, just how full of illusions our lives really are. I had spent the better part of that day on a spiritual retreat, reading scripture, praying, and writing, and at the end of it I turned on the television to watch the news. Instead of Bob Bordeaux and Melanie Lawton, two local TV news anchors, I got an Infiniti commercial suggesting something was wrong with me if I didn't buy or couldn't afford that car. A Crystal Pepsi commercial followed, suggesting that its product would transform me into a real "whizbang" with the ladies (which, unlikely as that seems in any case, wouldn't go over well with my wife). And that was followed by another and another and another until, finally, the news came back on.

Those commercials all had something in common, I decided upon reflection: they were all lies. We all know that, I suppose, but do you ever wonder what effect all those lies have on our psyches? Isn't there a proverb that says, "Repeat a lie often enough and it becomes truth"? What effect does all that lying have on children, who watch thousands of hours of that stuff before they ever realize that those things are lies? What does it do to us as a society to have our desires stroked and prodded so often, in the interest of selling us products that can't satisfy those desires to begin with? The newscast that night contained the answer to that question—rampant drug use, carjackings, murders, suicides, greed, and selfishness, all symptoms of desires gone crazy. Television was a self-answering question.

All of that reminded me of an ancient teacher who taught "Four Noble Truths" on the subject of desires. Truth One stated the obvious: our lives are filled with frustration and suffering. Truth Two located the origin of such suffering and frustration in our unlimited desires, eternally wanting what we cannot have. Truth Three offered the possibility of escaping such suffering by mastering the desires within us. Truth Four laid down an eight-fold path for going beyond desire: "right views, right intentions, right speech, right conduct, right livelihood, right effort, right mindfulness, right concentration." The day-to-day application of these four Truths makes it possible to get beyond the constant human yearning for more and more, to escape from that nagging inadequacy inside that keeps us in chains.

It dawns on me that people conditioned from birth to fulfill as many desires as possible may ask what the point of that would be. Why give up desires, or even make the effort to? And in asking that question, I realize that no abstract answer is sufficient. If we are happy being manipulated, then there's no reason in the world. But if, like the bad taste in our mouths that follows the ice cream cone, we have seen that all life's pleasures leave us unfulfilled, then perhaps we begin to see the answer.

To find peace in this world, inner peace at least, it is necessary to move beyond the constant compulsion to get, to have, to use. When we approach such peace, perhaps it is possible to understand why God created us to begin with...and surely it wasn't to watch Infiniti commercials.

And if that's what you're looking for, might I suggest you take a hard, faithful look at those four Noble Truths up there, and begin your search by turning off the television.

KEEPING BALANCE

I've noticed that persons who live their lives with particular intensity tend to focus on the big things in life and pay less attention to the smaller ones. This is neither surprising nor bad. After all, people blessed with much energy and enthusiasm generally want to accomplish a great deal—build up a business, grow a large church, make a difference in a community and beyond—and such persons need our encouragement. In the political realm, particularly, we need to encourage people of genuine energy and vision, regardless of party, to reenergize public debate and get things moving forward again.

But as we do this, we also need to remind them—and, I suppose, ourselves—not to neglect entirely the small in pursuit of the great. Large issues, after all, tend to be amalgamations of smaller ones. Large concerns become so because they touch many, many lives on a small scale. And if large solutions leave small concerns unaffected, those large solutions will fail, again perhaps as our present political situation indicates.

Learning to address large concerns means remembering they are made up of smaller ones, an insight that provides guidelines for our involvement in the world as well. You and I never know the consequences of our actions, whether or not, for instance, one small act of Christian virtue will have an enormous ripple effect beyond itself on those very larger issues that so concern us. Even though we may not think we are involved in great decisions, we should never discount how important the small things we do may wind up being. When we have the opportunity to do good on however small the scale, we need to do it.

There is an inner component in all this, too. Moral development doesn't happen on a large scale. Our character is shaped day by day, decision by decision, in small increments over time. We deceive ourselves if we think we can skirt the edges of truth in small things now and not pay a price when it comes to the larger things later.

Confucius, the great Chinese philosopher/politician, summed it up this way:

> If good does not accumulate, it is not enough to make a name for a man. If evil does not accumulate, it is not enough to destroy a man. Therefore the inferior man thinks to himself, "Goodness in small things has no value," and so neglects it. He thinks, "Small sins do no harm," and so does not give them up. Thus his sins accumulate until they can no longer be covered up, and his guilt becomes so great that it can no longer be wiped out.

Jesus said something quite similar: "Whoever can be trusted with very little can also be trusted with much; and whoever is dishonest with very little will also be dishonest with much." He took it a step further, reminding us to always ask where true worth is to be found: "So if you have not been trustworthy in handling worldly wealth, who will trust you with true riches?" (Luke 16:10–11, alt.)

We need to encourage right-hearted ambition, that sort of striving after great things that still manages to keep it all in perspective. Build your business, if that's what God leads you to do. Grow the church, if that's your calling. But however large your concerns become, remember they are made up of smaller ones. Be faithful and honest in those, pay attention to the details of moral formation, and you will meet the weightier issues truthfully as a matter of course.

We find true wealth, after all, not in bank vaults or stock markets, not among the rich and powerful as the world sees such things, but in the presence of the living God who has called us to do justice, love kindness, and walk humbly in God's presence.

Maintaining Perspective

It's easy to lose perspective, isn't it? In our spirits there seems to be an eternal conflict between our optimistic impulse and our pessimistic one, between a brighter hope for the future and depression. Because we're mortal, our pessimism is natural. What we are sometimes tempted to forget, though, is that as God's children the hope within us is more than natural.

All of us, I'm sure, go through times when we seem to have lost our way. Perhaps we get into a fight with a spouse, friend, or loved one. The fight then expands in our minds until it infects everything we do. Maybe we receive bad news—about our health or the health of someone close, about our jobs, or the like. Worries about these things, too, can grow to all-consuming proportions inside us.

It's futile to address such worries with platitudes. We can't just say to ourselves or to others "snap out of it," or "just stop worrying." At least, we can't if we're honest with ourselves. There are times when conflict is too strong, distress too deep, worry too profound to respond to superficial prescriptions. Paradoxically, we are healthier when we admit such problems are larger than we can handle instead of trying to keep a brave face on things.

What strength can we draw on when the downside seems to get the better of the upside? Of course, Christians, we can draw on the strength of our faith. Yet how can we keep faith's strength from being just another platitude? "God will take care of it" can be as hollow as "snap out of it" if we're not careful. Faith is more than a platitude when it forms the foundation for our outlook on life, and that can happen only when we practice it daily.

The basics of faith are meaningful when they become part of who we are. It means so much more than most of us realize to know that in Jesus, God has shared the same struggles we face. Jesus knew what it meant to lose loved ones. He knew about uncertainty. He certainly drank to the dregs the cup of suffering and death we too share. In all our struggles God is with us. Not only that, faith assures us that God triumphs over these things, that out of the birth pains of suffering in this world, the kingdom of God is born.

This is an anchor when our perspective wavers. It keeps us upright and reminds us where we can place our trust. Yet there is a cautionary note in it, too. The time to cultivate faith is not during the hard times, but during the good times. God strengthens us a little at a time, through a lifetime of devotion. If we wait to the last minute, we likely will have waited too long.

So, friends, knowing that we will face tough times—whether today or some day hence—begin laying up your treasure in God's presence today. One constant in this life is change, and unless we are anchored in the One who does not change, we will be swept away. Cultivating our faith may seem like an optional activity until the crunch comes. How terrible to wait until then, discover how much we need faith, and find it's not there to call upon.

Don't let that happen. Make conscious, daily efforts to pray. Set aside time to read your Bible. Come to church faithfully. And through these things God will strengthen you until the day dawns when we all stand in God's presence with rejoicing.

The Anger-Eating Demon

Once upon a time, a demon sneaked into the throne room of heaven and sat down in God's place while God was in another room. Even though it was a sickly, scrawny demon, heaven's citizens were outraged by its impudence.

"What do you mean sitting down in God's chair?" shouted one of the angels. "Who do you think you are?"

But when the angel finished shouting, to his immense chagrin he saw that the sickly demon grew larger. This further enraged some of the saints standing nearby, who could no longer hold in their anger and began to scream at the demon also. "What makes you think you can do that? Only God is allowed to sit in that chair! We would never do something like that!"

When the saints finished shouting, to their immense chagrin they saw that the demon had grown larger still. This, in turn, enraged the archangels seated nearby, and they began to shout at the demon, "If you don't get out of that chair this instant we'll call Gabriel and he'll throw you out and back down to hell where you belong!"

In fact, all heaven's citizens were so angry that they gathered around the demon on the throne and screamed at it with all their might. Yet with every shout and for all their anger, the demon only grew larger and stronger. By this time, in fact, he was no longer a sickly, scrawny demon. He had become a huge, fearsome, imposing demon, so that even the angels began to fear him.

At this moment, God came back in. Instantly, all heaven's outraged citizens turned to tell God of the outrage the demon had done. "He's in your chair! Tell him to get out! Throw him into hell where he belongs! You can't let him get away with this!"

God, however, motioned the others out of the way, went up to the throne, and knelt before the horrifying apparition that now occupied it. "Peace to you, anger-eating demon," God repeated. "Peace to you."

With each word, the demon shrank in size and fearfulness, until, with the third repetition of the phrase "Peace to you," it vanished without a trace, and God resumed God's rightful place.

Peace to you and to all your demons!

Died for Us?

Modern Christians often have difficulty accepting that Christ had to die for our sins. Sacrifice is not a part of most of our daily routines, and thoughts of sin less so. We are conditioned to think not in terms of giving things up in order to improve our condition, but on acquiring things to do so.

Yet the New Testament teaches plainly that Jesus died for our sins. "For I handed on to you as of first importance," Paul writes, "what I in turn had received: that Christ died for our sins in accordance with the scriptures" (1 Corinthians 15:3). From Jesus' own lips comes the statement, "The Son of Man came not to be served but to serve, and to give his life a ransom for many" (Mark 10:45).

What are we to make of this, then? In contemporary "mainline" Protestant churches, we don't make much of it at all. We don't talk about sin, much less concern ourselves with its seriousness. In fact, we often find such talk offensive. Not wanting to offend, but wanting to be accepted and popular, we ignore the subject and scoff when it comes up.

Perhaps we can be persons of faith without taking seriously the notion of sin, but can we be persons of Christian faith that way? The Bible entertains no illusions about our sinlessness. "All have sinned and fall short of the glory of God" (Romans 3:23). "If we say that we have no sin, we deceive ourselves, and the truth is not in us" (1 John 1:8).

Curious that we should reject that teaching today, isn't it? One might well wonder how a century that has witnessed global war, genocide, totalitarianism, and mass starvation could think itself sinless. Perhaps it's that we think only others have sinned. "Those people have, not me." Look in your heart and I will look in mine—can we really say that?

According to the Bible, human sin is serious business. We who have seen the bodies stacked like cordwood outside extermination camps in Poland and Cambodia, who have witnessed the starvation of children in Africa while food rots here, who have watched rivers and streams turned poisonous by rampant pollution, who see the homeless on our streets every single day ought to know about that. Our denial itself is sinful, and sin is serious, serious business. It is a cancer that, if left unchecked, will destroy each of us.

And like cancer, treating it involves suffering. Just as cancer patients suffer through chemotherapy in hopes of healing, so humanity suffers in hopes of salvation. We must sacrifice to live. And Jesus of Nazareth is our sacrifice—the one who bears our sins on the cross so we might be forgiven. He makes possible a healing that otherwise is impossible.

Here's our dilemma. Like many forms of cancer, sin can be overcome if we are willing to accept treatment. Like untreated cancer, sin will kill us if we don't. To accept the treatment that heals is to accept what Jesus has done for us and to live as Jesus would have us. Neither is easy to do. Both change us to the core of our being, oftentimes in pain. Yet without that change, we die.

May we believe and live.

Pain Too Deep for Words

There's no getting around it. Sometimes things break and there's just no fixing them. We can kick and scream, cry and resist, but all the tears are in vain. My mother cultivated a miniature pine tree when I was a kid. It always stood by the sliding glass door, a mini-holy of holies that ranked right alongside her special lamp on a short list of things kids weren't to touch. We all have such lists, I suppose.

She entered that tree in a competition every year, finishing second each time behind the same person. Second isn't bad, of course, but she wanted that first prize trophy. One year she got together with the lady who owned the *numero uno* tree before the big competition. Somehow the lady agreed to hold off that year, not enter the contest, and my mother came home sure of victory.

The day before the big event my brothers and I had a furious pillow fight in the den, too close to both tree and special lamp for comfort. I still remember taking careful aim at Stuart and letting fly, only to see him dodge at the last instant. I then watched in horror as the pillow I'd thrown sheared six limbs off my mother's prize tree the day before the big competition.

In moments like that, a kid almost wants to get punished. I expected all heck to break loose and felt so doggone bad I really didn't mind. But, to my immense puzzlement, no harsh words were said. Nobody yelled. My backside remained unpaddled. My mother mumbled something about things hurting too badly to say anything, but at the time I didn't know what she meant.

Sometimes things break. We're distracted, involved in the pillow fight we call life. At a particular moment we let fly at something or someone, only to have that person duck at the last minute. Then we watch our missile tear into something someone else values greatly. Then we watch as they suffer the pain words can't express.

Sometimes we're on the receiving end. It's our miniature tree, our cherished dream, our relationship that breaks. In an instant, or sometimes over a period of years, all the careful cultivation is brought to nothing. What had been a beautiful tree becomes a piece of refuse.

After all these years I know about those pains that are too deep for words. Such pains are part of the core curriculum in the school of hard knocks, a school you and I have enrolled in simply by being born. We'll face them, no question about it.

The question is what we'll do about them. All too often the temptation is to focus entirely on what has been broken and to lose sight of everything else. Without trivializing the pain, I've learned that focusing on the loss alone doesn't help. We don't have to pretend the break doesn't hurt; we just have to remember there's more to life than the brokenness.

In the midst of brokenness, I find it helpful to remember that which cannot be broken. Thomas Merton talked about the "still point" within, the place where God is, where brokenness is transformed. God's saints—people like you and me—find shelter there even in the worst of times. They don't do this to hide from the world or from brokenness. They do this because they trust God, for whom nothing is ever irretrievably broken.

Things break, no doubt about it. Look for the one whose love never breaks.

Fragments

Once upon a time, rumor has it, there was a wondrous mirror that shone with such utter clarity that all who looked into it could see themselves and the whole universe just as it was. It sparkled with stars, planets, living things, people—all the beauty of the world—yet even that was not the whole of the story. It is said that when one looked at it with just the right frame of mind, one could see beyond the objects reflected in it to the very face of God. Nothing like it has ever been recorded, either before or since.

Yet this is only a rumor, of course, because no one alive remembers seeing the mirror in one piece. All that's left of it are fragments, broken pieces, but since even those fragments are priceless it seems logical to think the whole mirror was even greater than the sum of its parts.

Each fragment offers a unique perspective on God, the world, and the observer, and each has proven powerful, almost hypnotic over time.

Unfortunately, the fact that each fragment offers a slightly different perspective on things has been the cause of terrible quarrels through the years. The problem arose because the mirror's fragments became scattered geographically. People of one village would look into the one they possessed, become captivated by the beauty it revealed, and decide with absolute conviction that they alone had the True Image. When such folks heard people from other villages describe the True Image differently, it was not at all uncommon for them to become terribly upset, even to the point of violence. After all, when people are convinced from their hearts that they are right, it's hard to accept someone who sees things differently.

The earth is a big place, however, and for a long time the possessors of the different fragments were able to keep their distance from each other. Only on the borders between them or when small groups of people who saw it one way were surrounded by large groups of those who saw it another did the conflict continue to erupt. One side would shout, "I have seen this thing with my own eyes! I know it looks exactly like this! How can you say it doesn't?" Oddly enough, the other side would usually shout exactly the same thing.

At times, the conflicts grew so bitter that some people decided the fragments themselves were the problem, making up their minds to have nothing to do with such mumbo-jumbo in the future. But those folks couldn't escape the conflict so easily. The only thing worse than looking into these wondrous yet dangerous mirrors was not looking into them. Human life just ceased being human at that point.

So life went on and the world got more crowded and the different peoples found themselves living side-by-side whether they wanted to or not. Over time, three schools of thought concerning the mirrors arose. Those who wanted nothing to do with the mirrors were quite common, empty though their lives seemed to be. Those passionately committed to their own fragment, certain that it alone was valid, were also common.

Yet among them both as a tiny, despised minority were those who had actually taken the time to look into more than one of the fragments. The experience was unsettling for them because the True Image really did look different when seen through different mirrors. But over time the conviction had grown in these people's hearts that each image was true in its own way. They were forced to open themselves to the fact that, beautiful as their native image was, it was only partial. They found themselves longing to be able to reconstruct the whole mirror and see it in its totality. Their approach did not make them popular, but they held to it as if the very future of the world was at stake.

May we each bring our fragments together in love!

Great-Grandmother's Yard

The trees in my great-grandmother's yard in Longview seemed immense when I was a child. The house itself was imposing enough: a covered portico off the driveway, my great-uncle's workshop off the garage, a paneled office inside, and then the great central staircase to the bedrooms. On either side of the stairway were two rooms, holies of the holy really, filled with elegant furniture and definitely off-limits to children. Those rooms gave the whole house an air of mystery and grandeur.

The front door was at the foot of the stairs and served as the portal to the great trees. For the life of me, I can't remember ever coming in through that door—we always came in the back—but it was the "front" door nonetheless. And at least once during the visit someone, usually my grandmother when she got tired of the noise three boys can generate, would open the mysterious door and usher us kids out into the yard.

It was always rather awe-inspiring. The trees towered up into the heavens, an old swing hanging from the lowest branch of the one closest to the house. Highway 80 roared away at the end of a huge expanse of lawn. My brothers and I played football or freeze-tag out under those trees under Grandma's watchful eyes. Sometimes, though, when the leaves were falling and a crisp breeze was in the air, we'd just sit there and imagine we were in the grandest place in creation.

Great-grandmothers by nature don't linger long in the lives of little children, and mine passed when I was eight. We kept going up to the house for a few years, but we finally severed ties and sold it. I probably hadn't seen the house or the trees in a decade when my Dad and I finally made it back last winter. Needless to say, it had all changed. The neighborhood had filled up with cheap businesses. The spacious, country feel was long gone. And the trees looked, well, ordinary. It was no loner the grandest place in creation.

To tell you the truth, the changes weren't unexpected. Almost all of us have experienced them—not changes so much in the external environment but in the way we see it. What loomed large, even magical, through childlike eyes now has grown ordinary, almost forlorn, with our weary maturity. It has happened to us so often that it has become the expectation: we come to expect our lives to be empty of wonder, so thoroughly have we trained ourselves not to see it.

Yet I had a dream the other night that reminded me where the wonder comes from. I was out under those trees again; they were as marvelous as I remembered, and yet I was big, not little. I puzzled over it in the dream, wondering why everything seemed so much brighter than it had seemed last winter. At that moment, I realized wonder is not a property of the world around us, but of our hearts.

I discovered I couldn't shut that realization out the next day, even after I awoke. I went out to get the paper in my own front yard as I always do, but I took the time to look up and wonder at the great oak tree that stands there. Coffee in hand, I went into the girls' bedroom and marveled over them as they slept. I was once again in a magical world.

It occurs to me now that God intends for our capacity for wonder to be lifelong. Jesus once said, "Unless you come as a little child you will never enter the kingdom of God." I think I finally know what he meant.

When we can wonder, any old yard becomes the grandest place in creation.

Wanting Something *For* Us

There is a great difference between loving someone because we want something *from* them and loving them without expectation, simply because we want something *for* them. I confess to having thought of love in terms of what the loved one could do for me. I felt a void inside and expected my loved one to fill it. I had low self-esteem and thought my lover would raise it. I needed pleasure and satisfaction and I looked to the human object of my desire to fulfill those things. Love was not about the other person, but about me: my needs, my insecurities, my longings. I blush a little admitting that publicly, but all of us have probably loved in such a way. We live in a culture that teaches us to ask first and foremost, "What's in it for me?"

But my four years of parenting have opened up for me an entirely new way of loving. I don't find myself thinking of my girls in terms of what they can do for me. What their mother and I concern ourselves with more than anything else in life right now is what we want for them, not from them. We want for them the ability to live life well, to form deep and meaningful friendships with others, to make positive contributions to the world in which they live. We want them to have an anchor in values that transcends selfishness, to have root in the love of the One who has brought them into life and being. And for this, we're willing to sacrifice whatever we have to, because nothing else means as much.

This has helped me see my own upbringing in a new way. Too often these days, our victim-oriented society encourages children to focus on what our parents did wrong. I see with increasing clarity these days all the many things my parents did right! I remember their positive presence at the important moments in my life: watching my brothers and me play football, attending our school plays, supporting us in our chosen endeavors. They chose to be with us, though no one compelled them to be. We always had at least two fans in the stands whose presence said, "We love you." The fact that not everybody had that makes it all the more precious.

And that's the way it is with God's love also. Too many times, when we think of God at all, we think only of God's demands. Yet God has given us commandments, not because God wants something *from* us, but because God wants something *for* us. "I come," Jesus said, "that you may have life and have it abundantly." God wants for us what parents want for their children, and the commandments are a gift to us to help us realize that. The hallmark of God's relationship with us is presence: God is with us, through good times and bad!

Over time, that becomes more and more important. We all reach points in life where we need a friend who will love us even in the darkest moments. What comfort it is to realize we have such an advocate who will be with us to the end! Receiving that kind of love empowers us to give it more freely to others.

I pray that each of us will cultivate an appreciation for this God who is our ever-present help in times of danger, who loves us with all the passion of parents who by their mere presence help their children become what they can be. That's the God we worship.

Happy Mothers' Day to one and all!

The Goodness of God

Funny, the way we test God's goodness. Isn't it almost always in terms of whether the things in our lives seem pleasant or not? If God is good we will have smooth sailing, or so we think. And if our lives become rough and painful, then obviously something must be wrong with God. Faith in God should mean, we tell ourselves, that only good things happen to us.

Of course, we know that is unrealistic, yet I wonder how many of us somehow expect it anyway? Certainly the people of ancient Israel—God's "chosen ones"—had such expectations. When they were building their empire under David and Solomon, they saw the favor of God behind their success. Their prophets spoke ecstatically of a Davidic reign that would never end. "There will always be someone on your throne" they told a grateful king.

Yet their empire fell apart, as all empires ultimately do. And when it did, their faith in God was shaken to the core. The writer of Psalm 44 cries out to God about this injustice: "Now you have rejected us; you don't lead us into battle, and we look foolish....All this has happened to us though we didn't forget you or break our agreement. We always kept you in mind and followed your teaching. But you crushed us, and you covered us with deepest darkness."

If success was a sign of God's favor, what in the world did failure mean?

A modern historian, of course, would look at Israel's ancient empire and find an entirely different set of reasons for both its success and its failure. It rose to prominence during a period of Egyptian and Assyrian weakness. The empire may well have lasted longer had it remained united politically, but its internal divisions soon tore it apart. When Egypt and Assyria, the two "superpowers" of the day, revived, a divided Israel soon became another victim. The modern historian can be forgiven for thinking God had very little to do with it at all.

If God does not favor one people over another or intervene in human affairs on behalf of a chosen few, what can we say about God's goodness? Worldly success has a lot more to do with wealth and cunning than with faith and sincerity. If you don't believe that, just look at our presidential campaign. So where is God in this? Even ancient Israel realized there was no easy answer to this.

I believe God is an inner reality, the source of life and the standard of beauty and goodness. I believe God shares Godself with every living creature, without a shred of selfishness. We each receive just as much of God as we are ready, willing, and able to receive. Yet God does not play favorites, as Peter plainly said in Acts, and God does not manipulate human events to favor one group over another.

To come to grips with the reality of God, we have to see beyond our own narrow interests. We can't judge the goodness of God solely by what happens to us, to our nation, to our religion, or to those we love. As Paul said, "Time and chance happeneth unto all."

I am coming more and more to believe that the only way we will ever know the goodness of God is to give up our attachment to the world outside us, to accept life with all its ups and downs, and to focus our attention on the God who lives within. We have to "die to the world," to use the ancient image, in order to live to God. Once we begin doing that, though, once we look within and commune with the Reality who makes us, we discover a goodness, a love, that no external circumstance can ever diminish.

Look for it until you find it, my friends in Christ.

Seeing as God Sees

I remember standing on the playground as a child, waiting as the teams were picked. The class had two permanent captains, the best football players in the fourth grade. I wasn't one of them.

It seemed like I was always the second person picked and that my team always wound up losing. It galled me to be picked second. I wanted to be first more than anything else in the world. It just never seemed to happen.

Looking back on it, it occurs to me that I never even thought about those picked "lower" than me. I never had the experience of hanging at the back of the crowd, waiting and waiting, being the last one chosen. And it never would have occurred to me then to be anything but contemptuous of those who weren't picked higher than me.

It was a pecking order, small and petty as it was. Being picked second conferred status, though not the status being first would have offered. But I took my little parcel of status and used it to separate myself from those I didn't consider my equals. As Henry Kissinger once said, "The politics were so vicious because the stakes were so small."

Wouldn't it be nice to think we grow beyond that kind of pettiness? Perhaps we can conceive of a world where even the last ones picked have equal value with the first. Conceive of it, yes. Live in it? Who knows.

The fact of the business is that we don't grow out of such competitiveness with age. We just tend to play the game on a higher level. And those who are involved in it up to their necks still look with disdain on those hanging on the edges of the crowd, those picked last if at all. Isn't this the way the world is?

Yes, but there are other ways of seeing things. Chuang Tzu, an ancient Chinese philosopher, mocked the blindness of his own society by telling the story of Wu, the hunchback. Wu was terribly deformed, at least in the eyes of his fellow villagers. They felt pity for him even in the midst of their disgust.

When food was short, they always saw to it that Wu received a double share. When the governor came by to round up labor parties, Wu was never included. When the young men of the village went off to war, Wu stayed home. Such pity.

Yet one by one Wu's contemporaries wasted themselves and their lives, working too hard or dying in the war. Wu was perfectly capable of tending his own farm, making his own living. While the others were looking down on him, making him the object of their "charity," Wu was quietly getting rich. He died an old man, Chuang Tzu pointed out. Who was the unfortunate one?

How about the way God chooses? Isn't it ironic that Jesus was born literally in a cow stall, among the riffraff of an enslaved people? No pomp and circumstance there, unless you count cows chewing cud an act of celebration. What a pity to have a baby there, instead of in some nice clean Roman villa or a modern hospital.

Yet the refrain echoes throughout the New Testament: "God chose what is weak in the world to shame the strong. God chose what is low and despised in the world, things that are not, to reduce to nothing things that are, so that no one might boast in the presence of God" (1 Corinthians 1:27–29).

Perhaps our standards are wrong and our pity misplaced. I hope I can come to see those around me the way God sees them, in hopes that God will see me with love as well.

Who Prays for Us?

The story in Exodus 32 reveals the depth of the crisis. Israel, having been delivered from slavery in Egypt, seems to have doubted at every turn the One who delivered them. Now, in Moses' absence, they have turned away from God entirely and made for themselves a golden calf, symbolic of their longing for a suitable homeland.

God, much like the parent of an unruly teen, has had enough. In effect, God says, "Get out of the way, Moses! I'm going to let 'em have it once and for all!"

"Now, God," Moses remonstrates, "if you do that, you'll get a bad rap among all the other peoples. Don't kill them all, or people will say you brought them out of slavery but couldn't make a nation of them." God in the end relents, and the people live to sin another day.

The story has always amused, puzzled and challenged me. It's an interesting portrait of God and a fascinating role reversal for Moses. The impudent can be forgiven for wondering if God was having a particularly bad day that day, much like a mother with children who really get under her skin. Is God really like that, or was God just testing Moses to see what he would do in the crisis?

Yet apart from the strangeness of divine behavior in this instance, a deeper question comes out of the text on closer reading. Suppose we are Israel, that the story isn't just about something long ago and far away, but about us. Suppose we are the ones whose hearts are hardened against each other and against the One who sets us free. Suppose this story, so incomprehensible from a distance, is finally describing you and me.

Then, suppose God does get exasperated with God's people. Is this without reason? Do we live lives worthy of the calling we have received? Have we laid aside our irrational prejudices, our hatreds, our pettiness in embracing the all-embracing love of God? Do we work at loving all God's people, however different from us they may be, or do we also make for ourselves idols to comfort us at the expense of the One who truly can comfort?

If that describes us, then God is rightly exasperated. If we've thumbed our noses at the freedom we've received in order to enchain ourselves again to the works of our hands, then God's wrath is just, God's frustration is justified, and our suffering is understandable.

If this describes us, I wonder who plays the role of Moses for us today? Who looks at God's failing, faltering people not with eyes to judge but with a heart to forgive? When we have proven for the umpteenth time our utter unworthiness of the grace we've received, who prays for us? Let's hope someone does!

Yes, scripture tells us elsewhere, someone does pray for us. A millennium and a half after the Exodus, the apostle Paul saw clearly just who that someone was and is. "Likewise" he writes, "the Spirit helps us in our weakness; for we do not know how to pray as we ought, but that very Spirit intercedes with sighs too deep for words" (Romans 8:26). Exodus posed the question in its simplicity. Paul answered it. God's own Spirit prays for us.

That being so, perhaps we need to join in that work and pray for each other. I don't believe in magic, but I've seen too many times in my life where the power of prayer has made a difference. Even if I can't explain it, I certainly do believe it.

And believing it, I'm putting it into practice. Yes, like Israel of old, we have fallen short. Yes, God has every right to be impatient with us. And yet God's impatience is tempered with love, and God's own Spirit prays on our behalf. I pray for you, too, friends, and I hope you pray for me.

Why?

The question of Why? has troubled people of faith from the beginning. As Rabbi Kushner's famous book title put it, "Why do bad things happen to good people?" If God is both all-powerful and good, as we Christians proclaim, why is there suffering in the world? We all know from personal experience, some more intensely than others, that such pain is a reality in our lives.

As mature people, we expect some degree of suffering: we are mortal, after all, and death eventually comes to all. Yet if death's shadow crossed our lives only in its season, only when life had been lived long and fully, it would be easier to deal with. The crux of the question, the gut-wrenching aspect of it, arises when that shadow touches us or those we love out of season, while life is new, when the loss seems such an inordinate waste. Those times life wrenches that "Why?" from our insides with all the power of a sledgehammer. Why, indeed?

The answer is never, ever, either easy or simple. The first thing for us to remember in such circumstances is never to reduce to a platitude the answer to that question. How terribly hurtful it can be to say to someone in their moment of grief, "It was God's will." God's hand is never absent in any circumstance, of course, but a loving God does not willfully cause sorrow and heartache.

In the course of time, those grieving may indeed get to a point where they can see how God was working with them in that grief. They may even be able to resign themselves to God's wisdom in the face of tragedy, over time. But that insight is theirs to gain or not, in their own time. Throwing it at them prematurely only intensifies the pain.

How do we answer the question, then, of Why? First of all, we answer with a respectful, silent presence. We're simply there as the grief surges, doing what we can without philosophizing or theologizing inappropriately. Perhaps that silent yet tangible love will be the longest-lasting lesson grief teaches. As we attend to the grieving, without making demands, without trying to answer the as yet unanswerable, so God attends to us.

Then, at the appropriate time, we acknowledge that tragedy is part and parcel of human life. In this world there is no light without shadow, no joy without sorrow. We can't have one without the other, and if we would delight in life's blessings, we must accept life's burdens as well because "Time and chance," as the apostle Paul wrote, "happeneth unto all." The only remedy for tragedy is to remove ourselves so totally from all that gives either joy or sorrow that nothing touches us. That seems too high a price to pay even to avoid life's heartbreaks.

Third, we acknowledge that our human perspective is not the only, or perhaps even the final, one. "Now we know *in part*," Paul said. Our vision frays at the edges, overwhelmed at times by tragedy, but even in tragedy we have recourse by faith to the One who goes beyond tragedy. Partial as our vision is, it does not see just the bad. It also sees beyond to the form of the Resurrected One whose promise is eternal life. When our vision has been made complete by God, "then we will know *in full,* even as we have been fully known."

Our task in this as in everything else is to trust, even in the face of tragedy. Our God is good and all-powerful. Trusting that, I trust also that God does not allow anything to happen that can truly threaten those God loves. When the mist of tragedy clears and we see the Holy One face to face, we will understand that in full.

WHATEVER HAPPENED TO MIRACLES?

After one of my first efforts at teaching adult Sunday school years ago, a friend asked me, "Why don't we see miracles today the way they did in the Bible?" That's a good question and I couldn't answer it at the time. In fact, I'm still reflecting on it to this day.

Why no miracles today, if indeed there are none? Has God changed? Were the miracle stories theological inventions, as some would say? Does a materialistic age have no place for the miraculous? Is the distance between humanity and God so much greater now, that the deep faith from which miracles seem to have sprung simply no longer exists? Or are there miracles all around us that we simply do not see?

How we answer the question depends on what assumptions we bring to it. I personally don't believe God has changed or that all miracle stories are theological inventions. The Bible witnesses unanimously to God's constancy. One miracle—Jesus' feeding of the five thousand—comes to us from such a variety of multiple, early sources in the tradition as to warrant respect from even the most cautious scholars. It is better attested than any event in the life of Julius Caesar, than Caesar's life itself, but for some reason people don't question Caesar's historicity.

If God has not changed and miracles did happen once, why don't we see them now? Is it that we're too materialistic, too influenced by "secular humanism," too accustomed to believing only what we can see, hear, touch, or taste? Hardly. For all its alleged materialism, American society is capable of believing some pretty outrageous things. There just aren't many cold-hearted, materialistic, secular humanists left, despite what the fundamentalists say.

The answer seems to be rather complex, actually. There does seem to be a gulf between ourselves and God these days, at least in a lot of cases. Many of us practice "movie theater" religion. We drive to church, watch the show, and drive home, without ever imagining any personal connection between what we watch and our own lives. The characters in the stories we hear may seem vivid, but we interact with them only in the way we interact with characters in a movie. And people who talk back to movie characters are, in popular thought, either wacky, rude, or watching "The Rocky Horror Picture Show." Such an attitude does not provide fertile ground for the personal experience of miracles.

Yet there is more at work here than that. Perhaps our definition of miracle is too narrow. We've come to expect Charlton Heston "Ten Commandments"-style miracles, and in the process of looking for those we have missed the ongoing miracles around us. After all, the existence of intelligent life on a hunk of rock hurtling at fantastic speed around a small star doesn't seem like an everyday occurrence An earth that produces food of itself, bodies that regulate themselves, flowers that know when to bloom, and birds that know when to fly south don't seem run-of-the-mill either. Blinded by Cecil B. DeMille and Hollywood, have we missed what's truly miraculous in our world?

And I'm not so sure the other kinds of miracles don't still happen, either. It's just that they happen quietly, out of the spotlight, so we'll remember to put the focus not on the event but on God who brought it about. Ask people you know if they've ever experienced something miraculous—the answers will probably surprise you.

Why are there no miracles today? Who says there aren't? May God open our eyes to see.

Time's Winged Chariot

> But at my back I always hear
> Time's winged chariot, hurrying near...
> —Andrew Marvell

Maybe it's the gray creeping into the edges of the beard. Maybe it's the way people I treasure have disappeared out of my life, the sense that the years are accelerating. But lately I've definitely been hearing the steady beat of "time's winged chariot," and it raises interesting dilemmas.

Life has its stages, as we all know, and at the beginning of each we have to find our way anew. The ones before seemed to have such possibility, such promise. I couldn't wait to go away to school, for instance. I longed for the day when I could work in my profession full-time. I anticipated the birth of my children, though I don't think any of us can ever really imagine that before it happens.

My question is, what now? As I look around the culture, I don't really see many positive models for growing older and wiser at the same time. On those few occasions when I find myself watching television, I find I have no interest in the products being pitched at "middle-aged men" like myself. I don't feel a particular need for a sport-utility vehicle or Grecian Formula. I've been fortunate enough in my life to not feel that I'm lacking anything of substance, materially at least. I can't imagine a Subaru Outback commercial making me feel otherwise.

So again, the question is, what now? Our culture, idolizing youth and detesting age as it does, offers no answers. But not all cultures share such barbaric views. In fact, we swim very much against the stream of human history in the way we view growing older. As I've shared before, the ancient

Israelites treasured the wisdom that comes with age. It was "more valuable than silver and gold," they said, to be sought beyond all else. The Greeks, with their love of philosophy, also valued those lessons only time could teach. There's a similar respect for aging in most Oriental cultures as well.

Such an attitude isn't totally foreign to us either. George Burns, then pushing 90, once said, "My mother always taught me to respect my elders. The great thing about being my age is that I don't have to do that anymore. I don't have any more elders."

I'm sure the answer to "what now" won't come by frantically trying to forestall the inevitable. I'm not going to find it driving a red-hot convertible down Main Street with a beautiful young companion. The answer, if I'm to find it anywhere, will come from within, from a deepening wisdom, or it won't come at all.

And in a certain sense I suppose I'm ready for the exploration. I'm coming to a deeper awareness of what life is about, after all. I know much better now what things matter and what things don't. I've developed a healthy respect for life's surprises. I've tasted defeat enough to lose my arrogance, but won often enough not to count myself out.

Through it all, I've found God an utterly faithful companion. Oh, I admit sometimes that's not enough. Sometimes I want more than even God can give. But when the smoke of that wanting clears, God's always still been there—patient, waiting, inviting.

Whatever else loses its luster in the years ahead, I can only anticipate that deepening sense of God's love growing stronger.

May it happen for all of us.

Great Visions

Isn't it amazing how just a little bit of pettiness can take the steam off a great endeavor? This phenomenon is age-old, described by Chinese philosophers at least three thousand years ago. Yet it is still very much with us. How many times have we been in a group, planning, envisioning, scheming marvelous things, with all the energy and enthusiasm necessary to bring those things into being when, all of a sudden, someone stands up and says, "Well, if you ask me, it'll never work!"

Curiously enough, we hardly ever do "ask them," at least the kinds of "them" that are likely to insert enough pettiness into our vision to grind it to a blinding halt. They speak anyway, without invitation, and thus many a good idea has died aborning in business, in the church, in any organized endeavor.

Beware, friends, of those things that narrow our vision! It is a good thing to keep our feet planted on the ground and try to be realistic when it comes to our vision. It is not a good thing to have no vision at all because we're stuck up to our knees in the ground and so "realistic" we don't think we can do a thing.

If knowledge is power, a crucially important piece of knowledge for each of us is to know just where the nay-saying voices come from in our lives, whether in our lives together in community or in our personal lives. I find that in most groups, people already have a good idea about that. How many times do we see a roomful of people subconsciously cringe when someone stands up to speak? In spite of that, how many times do we let those voices have veto power over what we intend to do? Too many, I'm sure.

It's harder to keep a handle on those things in our personal lives. There, the voices of doubt and fear may masquerade quite effectively as prudence and good old-fashioned common sense. I heard the good old-fashioned common sense line a lot in my growing up years. "Don't dream those dreams, John—use your common sense." "Don't strive for that goal, John—you'll never make it." We hear those things so often that they become part of us. The hesitancy becomes built-in. And, as with all good self-fulfilling prophecies, the belief that we can't do great things yields a reality of mediocrity, just like the voices of doubt and fear would have it.

Yet God calls us to dream great dreams and pursue great visions. One sign of the messianic kingdom in the scriptures is that "Your sons and your daughters shall prophesy, and your young men shall see visions, and your old men shall dream dreams" (Acts 2:17). Don't you imagine there were people with Peter the day when the church was born who said to him, "Don't go out and preach, Pete. No one'll believe a beat-up old fisherman like you anyway." Aren't we glad he didn't listen to them?

When God's spirit guides us, the fact is there are no limits to what we can accomplish. We can have a vision of a full sanctuary and then go out and accomplish it. We can see ourselves breaking free of destructive habits and then do it. We can envision a life rich in meaning, growing toward God, abounding in joy, and then live it. All these things are within our grasp because, simply put, all these things are exactly what God wills for us. "I come," Jesus said, "that you may have life and have it abundantly!"

To experience that abundance, we have to crucify the voices of doubt and fear that hold us back! Beware the taming power of small fears and small minds! Let God's vision flower in us, now and always.

Waiting for Rain

This "waiting for rain" business has still got me thinking. As of today, Sunday, nature continues to tease us. Last night it got overcast and, wonder of wonders for Houston in June, we got a cool breeze. All the elements in place: it just doesn't rain.

While I still turn one wary eye toward the tropics, I may actually venture a prayer or two for rain this week...not for me, of course. No rain means no mowing, which is always okay in my book. But I'll ask a rain prayer for the farmers and ranchers in the surrounding counties and for the people whose commitment to green grass will make their water bill look like the federal deficit if it doesn't rain soon.

All this makes me wonder: in the best of all possible worlds is there ever a drought? I'm sure we've all played that "best of all possible worlds" game before. We sit back with a little time on our hands and wonder, "What would the world be like if it were perfect?" The big stuff we probably think we could iron out in a heartbeat. There would be no more illness and death, to start with. People would all live impossibly long and happy lives. Why, we wouldn't so much as stub our toes or, to paraphrase an ancient writer, "strike our feet against a stone."

There's a great little story about such a world in Greek mythology. Once upon a time, an intrepid soul managed to slip into the underworld and lock up Hades, the god of the dead. All the dead souls then went free, ostensibly their hearts' desire, and no one living could die. The reunions, of course, were joyous beyond belief. The first weeks of Hades' imprisonment went well, too, but then things began to go wrong.

A murder victim tracked down his murderer to even the score, but the score wouldn't stay evened. All those extra mouths to feed began to be a problem. People ate up all their food and had to scramble to find something to eat. Many got weaker and sicker, suffering so that they longed for death. Death, of course, was impossible.

In the end, the outcry—human and otherwise—grew so loud that Zeus, the chief god, was compelled to step in. He freed his hated brother Hades as the only way of restoring the proper balance of life *and* death. Apparently, it just wasn't possible to have one without the other.

In the best of all possible worlds can there be such things as droughts? Perhaps in some far corner of the universe, in some world beyond time, the answer is no. But in this world, real as it is, there are droughts—both physical and spiritual. There is suffering, the pain it causes, and the hard-won wisdom it elicits.

Would we abolish them if we could? Of course we would! Even if I wouldn't abolish them for everyone, I'd certainly abolish them when my loved ones had to suffer. Even that, however, remains beyond our power.

We can, however, attune ourselves to the One who has taken suffering upon himself, conquered it, and opened a way for us through it. Granted, that way is only open to us through faith: disbelieve and it disappears. The way doesn't exempt us from droughts and hardships. Hardest of all, we can't discover the way's comfort by just thinking about it: we have to plunge in, and take the risk, to find out if it's true or not.

It seems like a high price to pay, except for one thing: the drought comes whether we believe or not. The relief God gives is even better than rain.

Cut Flowers

I'm fascinated by the custom of sending cut flowers. Don't get me wrong, it's a good custom. Sending someone flowers as a token of love and esteem is a good thing. Flowers are beautiful and the people we love are certainly worthy of receiving them from time to time.

It's the cut flower that makes me wonder. A cut flower, while it may be beautiful for a while, is ultimately defined not by its beauty but by what it lacks. And for all it may have going for it, what a cut flower does not have going for it proves to be its downfall every single time. A cut flower has no roots. In the absence of roots it can only wither and die.

You have probably noticed by now that I have a passion for evangelism. For me, that passion has everything to do with cut flowers. So many people in our world are like cut flowers—they possess a beauty of sorts, but it's a doomed beauty, valuable for a season yet fated to become valueless with the passage of time. For all such people may possess—money, success, power, status—what they do not possess is ultimately all important. What is lacking, again, is a root.

The Bible presents us with the notion that our living root is the love of God. To be rooted in the love of God is to have within us the resources to endure in this life. Rooted in the love of God, knowing God's strength and trusting in it, we can weather life's storms. When the winds howl and the seasons rage, we can stand firm and face the trouble. As the psalmist says, "Greater is he that is in me than he that is in the world."

Persons who are rooted in the love of God possess an inner beauty. While superficial, cut-flower beauty fades with the passage of time, this inner beauty that comes from being rooted in God only deepens. Our faces may be lined and weathered, but our spirits retain their springtime freshness. This beauty time cannot rob. It is what Jesus called "the pearl of great price."

In a world of cut flowers, we see around us the fruit of humanity's desperate search for roots. We witness the anguish that arises from being cut off from one's roots. It is a terrible thing to long for something unnamable, to keenly feel a lack in our lives and yet not know where to look to fill that void. This is the human condition apart from the love of God. When we as Christians see that sort of pain around us, we have a loving obligation to share the good news about the one who is our root!

So in this cut flower world, we absolutely must take seriously the task of evangelism. In Jesus Christ, God's love is made known. To abide in Christ is to abide in God. He brings "life abundant" to those who trust him. It is not coincidental that the happiest persons in our society today, according to a Gallup poll, are not those who are rich or powerful but those who have an abiding and dynamic faith in God.

Evangelism isn't about numbers. It isn't about filling the sanctuary on Sundays. It isn't about giving cut flowers to a dying world. It's about sharing the one root without whom all our other endeavors are futile.

In this cut flower world, knowledge of whom our root is is too precious to keep to ourselves. Let's share this joyous knowledge with those around us so that together we may all come to know God's peace!

For Whom Do We Pray?

For whom do we pray? In the Sermon on the Mount, Jesus astounded both his contemporaries and ours with the following teaching: "You have heard that it was said, 'You shall love your neighbor and hate your enemy.' But I say to you, Love your enemies and pray for those who persecute you, so that you may be children of your Father in heaven" (Matthew 5:43–45). So how far does the circle of our concern extend? Most of us pray for ourselves. Many of us pray for our loved ones and friends. Still fewer pray for the church and the nation. Maybe some pray for the poor and the hurting.

How many of us pray for our enemies? How many of us bent the knee during the Gulf War to pray for Saddam Hussein, or regularly pause during the evening news to pray for drug-dealing killers, or take a moment at rush hour to pray for rude, reckless drivers? How many of us pray for the presidential candidate of the other party, or for our daughter's worthless husband? How many of us pray for our spouses, parents, or children when our wills clash so bitterly with theirs? That circle, I would guess, is small indeed!

Yet these are the very people for whom Jesus tells us to pray! Two immediate questions arise: (1) how do we pray meaningfully for our enemies, and (2) what possible good can come of it? To answer question one, we pray for our enemies by lifting them up into the presence of God. We simply imagine the love of God filling their lives and working changes in them only God can work. This doesn't mean we approve of what they do or wish them success in those activities that make them our enemies. It does mean we connect them in our minds with God, realizing that if we are to be so connected, they must be also.

What good does it do? Leaving aside the effect such prayer may have on them, let's consider the effect it has on us. Simply put, it's harder to hate someone we pray for. In lifting them up to God, it's easier to see them as human beings who struggle as we struggle, make mistakes as we do, and have needs as we have needs. Our enemies cease being monstrous when we pray for them. While that may complicate our dealings with them, the fact that it makes it harder for us to hate is a blessing. Hatred poisons the soul.

Further, praying for enemies puts the conflict between us in perspective. God is greater than either us or our enemies, and placing our enemies under God's care makes the conflict with them less all-consuming. God becomes the focus of our lives, rather than our conflict with them. Praying for our enemies makes it harder to think of them as enemies. Again, this prayer does not imply approval. It does make it easier for us to live in harmony with God, others, and ourselves, though, which is probably what Jesus had in mind.

Who knows what else it might bring about? If we sincerely prayed for our enemies, perhaps the level of general anger and frustration in our lives would decrease. We might be motivated to seek more peaceful resolutions to problems. We might learn to love more genuinely by understanding the difficulties others face. All these would be blessings. Fact is, we probably don't know what benefits would come our way from this sort of prayer because so few of us ever do it.

Let's try an experiment together. When you finish this article, spend a few moments in prayer, becoming aware of God's nearness. Then, name some of those with whom you've had conflict, toward whom you have hard feelings, and imagine that same presence filling them. Say whatever words of forgiveness you need to. Repeat that prayer several times in the next few days and see how your attitude changes. Take Jesus at his word and see if it doesn't lead to a deeper sense of peace, one that by changing your heart begins to change the lives of those around you. That will be a blessing indeed.

Birdbrains

We were on the beach, watching the sunset. They—the birds, that is—were gathered around a scrap of bread a former beachcomber had left behind, having themselves a bird feast, when all of the sudden, another bird flew in to join the festivities.

This, apparently, was more than the other birds could handle. They "flew off the handle," in a manner of speaking. First, they began screeching at the newcomer. Then they opened their beaks and flapped their wings at him. When none of those tactics worked, they finally just banded together and chased him off. I could hear them screeching off over the dunes.

As soon as they left, though, another bird flew in to eat the tempting supper they had been so eager to defend. All I could think, watching from my towel a few feet away, was, "What birdbrains!"

If only I'd studied Bird in college instead of French, I could have pointed out to them the flaw in their strategy. There was enough cast-off bread to go around. The newcomer who flew in brought with him only a bird-like appetite. What did they hope to accomplish by fighting with him and chasing him off?

"Well," the birds might have squawked, "at least he didn't get to eat our bread!"

"That's true," I would have chirped in response, "but neither did you."

Fact is, you just can't preach to birds. I should have known that, but I suppose we forget things sometimes. After all, no less a preacher than Francis of Assisi, the great, peaceful lover of all God's creatures, had tried and failed to preach to the birds. Francis had been run out of Assisi for being insane, after giving away his abundant possessions to the poorest of the poor in the town. The rich townsmen hauled him before the local bishop, wanting to burn him at the stake for heresy. The bishop wisely decided nothing could be gained from burning a lunatic to death and merely forbade him ever to set foot in his home city again.

So Francis went and preached to the birds. "Birds," he told them, "you are all God's creatures. God loves each of you. It doesn't matter whether your feathers are black or white or speckled, whether you are large or small, fierce or mild. God loves you and God feeds you. There is enough for each of you in the gracious mercy of God."

The birds apparently didn't believe him either. I wonder if it frustrated Francis, dealing with birds, seeing their rapacious greed, flinching at their short-sighted, stupid selfishness? I wonder if he ever felt like giving up, going back home, and trying to get all his possessions back? Apparently he didn't, because for all his struggles, there was a certain kind of bird that eventually heard what he was saying. We do remember him as Saint Francis, after all.

And I wonder further, if Saint Francis were to preach today to the birds in my heart, the birds in your heart, and say, "There's enough for all of us if you'll only be generous...God's grace feeds each of us...Each of us matters in the eyes of our maker...," whether we would open our beaks, squawk our hatred, and band together to drive him off, even if it meant someone else ate the feast we were unwilling to share.

There is enough to go around...if we'll share it. Will we?

May our hearts squawk generously in honor of our Lord.

"While We Were Yet Sinners..."

Their friends never understood why they loved the child so. The boy was a terror as a youngster. He never did what he was told. He fought constantly with other children and talked back to all adults, to his own parents' endless embarrassment. He even kicked his mother once, in church in front of everyone.

As he grew, things went from bad to worse. School was utterly unacceptable to him and, to no one's surprise, he made himself utterly unacceptable to the school. After a long string of suspensions and paddlings, he finally dropped out, shortly before he was to have been kicked out for good.

After that, the boy bounced around from job to job and began sinking into an abyss of drugs and alcohol. When his parents tried laying down the law, he packed his bags and moved out. For the next several years, they only heard from him when he needed money or when he needed someone to bail him out of jail.

Finally, his luck ran out. He was busted for dealing drugs. This time the police had him cold, and all the money his parents spent on legal help couldn't keep him out of prison. When the trial was over, his father's health finally broke from the strain, and the old man died thereafter. His mother's health grew frail, too, but because of the size of the legal bills she had no choice but to keep working.

Then, news came that the boy had contracted AIDS from injecting drugs, and he would be released. He was sick enough not to be a threat to society anymore, the State decided, and they didn't want to foot the bill for his illness.

He had no place to go. His old friends wanted nothing to do with him now that he was dying. He had no job to return to and no skills to support himself, even if his health had permitted him to work. In desperation at the thought of dying on the streets, he wrote his mother. "I have no one else to turn to," he pleaded with her. "I need a place to go. Please let me in."

Her friends said, "Shut the door in his face! After all he's put you through, you don't owe him anything."

Her other children said, "That person isn't our brother anymore! He killed our father! Let him back in this house and you won't see us anymore!"

The day before he was to arrive, the old woman lay awake all night, agonizing over her dilemma. Her other children had done so well. They had homes, families, lives, and careers. The thought of losing them was unbearable. Her son had hurt her so deeply, so often. She knew she didn't owe him anything. And yet, the thought of him dying on the streets, alone and utterly unloved, was more unbearable than anything she could imagine.

Take him in and lose her life; shut the door in his face and lose her soul. "Oh, Lord, take this cup from me," she prayed on her knees all night long.

Yet dawn came and with it the dreaded knock. She paused as she reached for the door, her life flashing before her eyes. Then she opened it.

"Come in, my son. Come in."

"While we still were sinners," Paul writes, "Christ died for us" (Romans 5:8). All praise to the God who says, "Come in, my children. Come in."

"I Don't Know"

I'm sure you've noticed how hard it can be to say, "I don't know." For me it's not just a matter of ego, really. It's that my five-year-old, Martha, is full of a million questions and will not accept "I don't know" as an answer.

We look at pictures of her baby days and she asks, "How old was I in this?" If I'm the least bit vague, she can't stand it. So even if I don't know I'll make something up, just to give her a little peace.

Sometimes I get around this by giving absurd answers. She'll want to know why she can't eat chicken nuggets for the third consecutive meal and I'll say "Because the grass is green." Fortunately she has a sense of humor, or at least humors me by laughing at such things.

The downside is that when I do give her straight answers, she sometimes hesitates to believe me. "I'll ask Momma," she says. I know good and well she says, "I'll ask Daddy" when Momma tells her some things too. Be that as it may, she won't take "I don't know" as an answer.

You and I are older than she is, our questions are larger, but we probably don't like hearing "I don't know" either. Certain situations in life call for clarity, for precise, accurate answers. When you ask the IRS auditor how much you owe, for instance, you don't want to hear, "I don't know."

When it comes to even larger questions, the need for certainty only increases. In my business, when people face tragedy and heartache, and when they want to know answers to questions such things raise, they don't want to hear, "I don't know." Sometimes, though, that's the only honest answer.

A Zen student, in anguish over his mother's death, asked his master, "What happens when we die?" The master, reputed to be the wisest man in Japan, answered, "I don't know."

The student, horribly offended, demanded to know why not. The master answered simply, "I haven't died yet."

I don't know what happens when we die either, not having died yet. I don't know all the time why bad things happen to good people. The certainty we want from such questions, the details we crave, are hidden from us. To say otherwise is to pretend.

But I do know God. I've met God in scripture, made God's acquaintance through prayer, seen God's face in the needs and compassion of others. And this I can say: at every point in my life so far, God has been faithful and good. I may have wandered and left God, but God has never left me. Again and again, I've turned my unworthy, sinful face toward God and found there God's matchless love. Something tells me this will never change.

So, I don't know what happens when we die. I don't know the reasons for all tragedies. But I do know God. I have every confidence that the God I know will prove good even in tragedy, even beyond death. I may not know the details...no one does, really. But I know the One who'll be there when those details come about.

Why do we find it so hard to trust this, to surrender ourselves to the God of endless compassion?

I don't know.

Heading for Home

The psychologist Milton Erickson grew up on a farm in the Midwest. One day during his youth, a neighbor's horse, fully saddled but riderless, came up to him while he was out in a pasture. Erickson didn't know which neighbor the horse belonged to, but he reasoned that the horse knew. This horse was not Mr. Ed. It couldn't tell Erickson in words where its home was. Erickson had to figure it out some other way.

After thinking about it for a minute or two, he decided that if he got up on the horse and kept it from getting distracted, it would walk home out of habit. Erickson mounted up but didn't take the reins. The horse started walking. When it began to get distracted or started to graze, Erickson would redirect its attention to the road and keep it walking. After quite a walk, the horse turned down a lane to a barn. The horse's owner, whom Erickson did not know, rushed out to thank him for bringing the animal home, marveling at the young man's ability to do that since he knew neither the horse nor the farmer.

In his later practice, Erickson never forgot about the horse. Something in us, he believed, knows where home is. Unfortunately, it may not be able to communicate it in words. Being wordy people, we lose the ability over time to listen to these nonverbal, inner communications. Like the horse, we get distracted and wander off. We can't put into words why we're so miserable; we just are.

Sometimes we hurt enough to turn for help. But to the helper, we're a lot like the horse in the pasture—saddled up, riderless, lost. Too often our helpers mount up and take us where they think we belong. They may fill us with religious dictums or psychological theories and think they've ridden us home. And for a while we may feel better. But if it's not really "home" for us, the pain will return, most likely with greater intensity.

We need to mount up and let the horse take us home, but how? The horse communicates non-verbally. We're confused by words. What do we look for in our own lives as signs that the horse is taking us home? I believe the answer lies in knowing the difference between joy and pleasure. The horse feels joy as it nears its home, but its pursuit of pleasure too often delays the journey. As long as it stays focused on the joy, it gets closer and closer to home.

Might that be true with us, too? We value joy for its own sake. My daughters bring me joy, for instance. We value pleasure for what it does for us. I take pleasure in a fancy meal. Pleasure is not unimportant, but if it becomes the thing we live for, we're in trouble. Pleasure comes to an end, simply put. Something in us knows where home is and communicates to us in the language of joy. Like the childhood game, the more joy we feel, the "warmer" we're getting. The less joy we have, the "colder" we are. Healing comes for us as we move in the direction of joy.

Doing so, we realize how often we put other concerns ahead of joy, things like ambition, success, image, money, and status. We convince ourselves these things matter, and they do, but only somewhat. None of them buys genuine love, for instance. None of them buys a beautiful sunset. None of them buys God's presence.

It finally comes down to setting them aside, letting go of the reins, and allowing the "horse" to take us home. That's not necessarily a glamorous way to live in this world, but won't there be a celebration when we get home!

Grandma's House

Grandma's house was a wonderful place, stretching out over three wooded terraces in the Oak Cliff section of Dallas. Though I haven't been there physically for years, it remains in my mind's eye as a place of refuge where we kids could go and just lose ourselves in a different world, unhurried and at peace.

My brothers and I built elaborate forts on one of the terraces, then spent hours plotting ways to blow them down. We dug out my Dad's old, rusty, wheel-less tricycle and rode it like maniacs down the driveway, often leaving parts of our hide behind when we crashed. Sometimes we stole out the back gate to raid the neighbor's bamboo stand or go rampaging through the neighborhood, and on hot days we'd turn the hose on each other and play in the sprinkler until our little hearts were content.

When we got bored outside (which wasn't often) or when it was just too cold, we'd stay in and color pictures or go rustling through old closets full of stuff my dad and uncle never got around to taking with them into their adult lives. Grandma hung the pictures at the top of the stairs and left them until they yellowed. We gladly redecorated her house every time we came over, and she never seemed to mind.

When the day ended, she'd always be there with a refrigerator full of cold Cokes, waiting at the door for her little tornadoes to make their way back in. She never seemed to mind the way we looked or the fact that we'd torn up the yard. She didn't seem to be in a hurry and didn't seem to mind letting kids be kids.

Looking back on it, I understand now that she wasn't in a hurry. That season of her life, the season of hustle and bustle, had passed and she had the good sense to let it go. I realize now she probably wasn't thrilled by the way we trashed the house and yard. But I also know now, in a way I knew intuitively then, that it was more than worth it to her to have us drink all her soda and tear up her yard just to have us around. I see that in the way my girls' grandfather, having passed the hurrying stage himself, tolerates their wholesale destruction of his house with nary a blink of the eye.

Even though Grandma and the world she inhabited have long since vanished from my life physically, I still go to her house in my mind's eye. I'm the one doing the hurrying now, the one making a way in the world and raising children, but I still remember with relish what it was like to be carefree, to go tearing down those familiar terraces as if there were no tomorrow. I have left childhood behind, but childhood has not left me.

And that's a comfort, too. We need places where we can go and be absolutely free and absolutely loved. I hope we have confidence enough in our imaginations to allow ourselves that luxury and not be held back by the thought that "This isn't reality." My grandmother is gone; someone else owns her house; but who's to say she's not more alive for me now than ever? She may not be in a physical place anymore, but isn't being human partly about being in touch with places beyond the physical?

In fact, I find my prevailing image of God these days has a lot more to do with what I remember about Grandma's house than with what I learned in seminary. I fully expect to find three terraces, a long driveway, and an old rusty tricycle in the yard when I get to heaven. And after I spend a long day screaming up and down that driveway on the trike, God'll be there by the door, Coke in hand, just happy to have the family together again.

Who Is That Lady?

The old woman didn't look very impressive when she walked through the door at Parker's Department Store. Her clothes were timeworn. The coat she wore was gray and faded, her hat perched precariously on an equally gray and faded head of hair. The salesclerk at the door didn't bother to interrupt his telephone conversation to greet her.

She went to the shoe department first. The salesperson there saw her coming, but waited until a younger, more fashionable customer walked up and served him instead. The old lady waited a few minutes, then went on.

At the makeup desk, one clerk snickered to the other as the woman approached. Her makeup was, to put it politely, out-of-fashion—too much lipstick, an absurd amount of rouge. Those clerks, too, waited on another customer first. Once again, the old woman stood there a moment or two hoping for help, then went on.

Finally, she went to the men's department where, once again, she was ignored by all. She picked out two pairs of men's socks and headed for the cashier's station at the front of the store.

The clerk there was still on the phone. He watched her approach the counter and said casually, "I'll be with you in a minute." Then he continued his conversation.

Again, she waited. After clearing her throat once or twice, she finally said politely but firmly, "Young man, I will be waited on."

The clerk, a "young man" only in comparison to her, flashed her an angry look and said, "Lady, I will be with you shortly!"

He then said to the person on the other end of the phone line, "Excuse me for a minute, but one of my customers just won't wait. I'll be back in a second."

He fixed the old woman with a savage stare and growled, "What do you want?"

She laid the socks on the counter.

"That'll be $5.50," the clerk snarled.

She reached into an ancient handbag and hauled out a credit card. Without so much as looking at it the clerk exploded. "We do not accept credit cards for that small a purchase! Why do you insist on wasting my...?"

He stopped in mid-sentence, mid-breath. She had placed the card down very deliberately in front of him, and he had read the name engraved on it: "Hilda Parker, Charge account #1."

She was the owner of the store.

Jesus said, "You also must be ready, for the Son of Man is coming at an unexpected hour" (Matthew 24:44).

Christ is in our midst. Are we ready?

Wide-Eyed Wonder

It's interesting the way our children teach us about life. Stereotypically, we parents are supposed to teach them, and we do, of course. Yet as in any teaching relationship, the learning is mutual.

My daughter Martha at age one looked at the world with wide-eyed wonder. To her, Planet Earth was a magical place, filled with totally unexpected sights and sounds and sensations. As she recognized some of its features, a little finger pointed to the night sky, for instance, and a delighted little voice shouted "Moon!"

As a matter of fact, she sees so much wonder and mystery in this (to our eyes) tired old world that even if I didn't know about God, I would suspect that God existed. What is divinity if not that sense of wonder to which children respond so immediately, without prompting—the wonder of a night sky, of a flower in bloom, of a white cat meowing at the kitchen window?

That the magic has gone out of these things for many of us speaks reams about our cynicism. It also explains why Jesus said, "whoever does not receive the kingdom of God like a child shall not enter it."

Children live unapologetically—embarrassed neither by tears when life hurts nor by exuberant laughter when it feels good. They also enable others to live that way, simply by being around them. Those who study such things tell us the presence of children in nursing homes has an amazing effect on many who reside there. But all of us who have delighted in watching children's sermons know that even before the experts tell us.

Of course, raising children is hard work. Some would say that the relationship between child and adolescent is like that between kitten and cat—more work but not nearly as cuddly. I don't necessarily agree with that, but I don't want to idealize either parenthood or childhood. All I do want to emphasize is the amazing effect seeing the world through uncynical, wondering eyes can have.

This matters particularly as Christmas approaches. Most of us have seen enough of "Christmas cheer" that the shine has pretty well rubbed off by now. Fighting the traffic, braving the malls, and spending hard-earned money hold less attraction than they once might have.

Yet deep down the wonder remains. It remains in the story of love, heroism, and redemption surrounding the birth of the Christ child. It remains in the ancient carols we sing in worship. It remains in the decorations, the music, the wondrous words of scripture. It remains above all in the memory of God in the flesh, in the thought that the Lord of heaven and earth experienced the world with the same wide-eyed wonder our children share now.

And, cynical as I often can be, I have never been able to sit through Advent worship services without the sense of wonder creeping back in. That, my friends, is what it's all about.

Thank you, children, for restoring our ability to marvel.

Stuck

Back in my days of playing wide receiver at good old Lakehill Prep, I had a recurring nightmare every season. I would line up, break over the middle on the snap, and catch a pass in the open field, nothing between me and the goal line but green grass. Since I was usually the fastest person on the field, it should have been a wonderful moment.

In the act of catching the pass, though, I accidentally stepped in the La Brea Tar Pits, and my feet stuck fast. All I could do was stand there and watch helplessly as the opposing team bore down on me at full speed.

For those of you who don't know, the La Brea Tar Pits are just that, great open pits of tar near what is now Los Angeles. Several thousand years ago, the tar pits trapped anything that strayed into them—buffalo, saber-toothed tigers, mammoths, and more. No matter how fast it moved, once it stepped in the tar pit, it stayed there for good. Eventually the tar dried, preserving everything that had been trapped in it. And if you wondered where those tar pits are now, they are right in the middle of the football fields I play on in my dreams.

Darn those tar pits! Just when I reached my moment in the sun, I'd step in them! All progress would halt instantly while the opposition closed in at full speed! If it weren't for tar pits, my football dreams would have been a lot more fulfilling.

Unfortunately, there are tar pits in other places, too. It's funny in a way, but sometimes the whole Christmas season now upon us seems like a tar pit. Maybe you know the feeling. We go into the season with such high expectations. After all, most Christian folk are genuinely moved to celebrate Jesus' birth. We also like to see family and friends, to share special moments with loved ones, and to give and receive presents.

Those things are like breaking over the middle in the game, wide open, and catching the pass.

But then we step in those dadgum tar pits! Between us and the end zone, task gets piled on task, duty on duty, obligation on obligation, until we discover deep down in our souls we don't have energy enough left to care about the Savior's birth or family or gifts. It's hard to get excited when you don't seem to be going anywhere.

And every year we hear the same warnings about holiday stresses, too. Pious voices join together as if in a litany to tell us: "Don't overeat; don't lose sight of what the season's about; don't get caught up in all the commercialism." And it becomes one big, sticky tar pit, with all the things we didn't get done rushing down on us like vengeful defenders.

It really doesn't have to be that way, though. In fact, I thought I'd use my immense authority as senior minister to give you some Christmas indulgences in advance this year. I give you permission:(1) to forget a couple of names on your Christmas card list and not feel guilty about it, even though they didn't forget you; (2) to politely hang up on a telephone solicitor asking you for money for another "good cause"; and (3) to miss one extra activity to stay home, drink eggnog, relax, and do nothing. By the authority vested in me, I declare you "not guilty" and authorize you to lighten up and enjoy yourself this year.

To paraphrase someone I admire greatly, the holiday was made for us, not us for the holiday. So take a little time off. Don't spend yourself into bankruptcy. Have at least one moment of genuine joy. Break into the open field and catch the Christmas pass.

Just be sure to watch your step.

Unopened Gift

I've seen kids do a lot of things with Christmas presents. They rip open the packages and play with some so fiercely the gift doesn't survive the week. Some gifts prove so annoying to parents that they mysteriously disappear before too long. I remember a couple of Christmases ago my brother gave Martha a talking alphabet toy that was so intriguing to his own children, they played with it the rest of the day.

After hearing that infernal machine respond to each push of a button with a flat, computerized voice, I did to my beloved brother probably the meanest thing of all the mean things I've ever done to him. As he and his girls got in their car to drive back to East Texas Christmas afternoon, I gave that toy to his daughters. Luckily, he didn't kill me or them…then again, I wasn't around four hours later when they got out of the car.

Kids greet some gifts with more enthusiasm than others. Some that aren't greeted enthusiastically at all—clothes, for instance—prove the most useful in the long run, particularly to parents on tight budgets. One thing I've noticed about every single Christmas present any kid gets: all of them get opened. Never once have I seen a kid leave an unopened present. Maybe that happens sometimes, but not in my experience.

Can you imagine such a thing? Say you're a beloved (or not so beloved if the kids remember last Christmas) parent, grandparent, brother, or sister. You go to a busy mall and select a present, bring it home, wrap it up, and put it under the tree. It takes time, effort, and a little imagination to do all that. What would you think if, after all that, the kid just looked at the package and put it back down unopened?

It's ironic in this season of giving and getting how many of us leave God's gift unopened under the tree. We may come to the celebration and open gifts from others, but the genuine gift we leave neatly wrapped under the tree. What gift is that? The gift of the gospel's power to transform our lives!

The reasons we do this are varied. Perhaps somewhere deep inside we fear that if we open this gift things won't be the same. We'll have to give up some things we cherish. We'll find ourselves led in directions we didn't want to go. Old friends may look at us differently. And as the warning label on the gift says, all those things are true! Yet the joy that comes with them all more than compensates for the changes, as all those who have opened it will testify.

Maybe we leave it unopened out of indifference. We've reached a point in our lives where we just don't care: about ourselves, about others, about God. We've let life's turmoil kill our capacity for joy. No one is happy in such a circumstance, but the paradox is that the very gift we're too indifferent to open is the only thing that can restore our joy.

Some don't open the gift because they don't know it's there. Most people in this world have no idea who Jesus Christ is and why his gift matters. Those of us who are "churched," as opposed to "unchurched," too often forget how many people don't know about this gift. What a thing to be ignorant of! Yet unless you and I tell them, how will they know?

As we celebrate Christmas this year, let's make sure we open all the gifts. One of those gifts—the gift of the gospel—will be the most wonderful we've ever received! And once we've opened it, let's make sure to give it to someone else!

Christmas Peace

It's the central idea of Christmas, the central paradox really. It's a mystery we have yet to come to terms with, despite two millennia of celebrating and misunderstanding Christmas and the miracle of Christ's birth. If this is the season of "peace on earth, good will toward all," why don't we have peace?

Of course, there are no simple answers to a question like this. Most of us would be hard-pressed to even define "peace," much less to know it if we saw it. Is peace merely the absence of war? If so, then Tacitus' comment on one of Caesar's wars might qualify: "He created a desert and called it peace." Hardly.

Is peace a question of justice, economic and otherwise? If so, then the lack of peace is hardly surprising. At the risk of sounding like a bleeding heart, I'm tired of seeing privileged young things in their Lexuses whizzing past homeless mothers and children in our city. Something in me cries out for justice when I see that, even at the risk of peace. Doesn't it with you, too?

It's hard to find peace, especially when we can't even define it. Let me hazard a definition, then. Peace is not necessarily the absence of war and conflict. It is not necessarily economic and social justice. It includes such things, certainly, but can't be reduced to them. If it could, Russian communism, which imposed domestic "harmony" through terror and economic "justice" through universal poverty, would have been a recipe for "peace." Hardly.

Peace is a mindset, an attitude, a conviction. It grows out of a profound insight that each human being is uniquely valuable. It carries with it the realization that we have no right to harm another, regardless of circumstances. And it spreads from a regard for human rights to a concern for the rights of all living things, a striving for harmony with the God of life.

The opposite of peace is not war but idolatry. We substitute gods of our own making for the God of life. We worship money, power, status, institutions, pleasure. And at these altars we sacrifice those who disagree or, more likely, those who simply get in the way.

Yet Christmas reminds us that God comes to us not as an idea, not as an institution, not as an imposing and distant monarch. God comes to us as a baby. God comes to us helpless, vulnerable, dependent. At Christmas we remember that our obligation to God is mutual. God doesn't just nurture us. We must nurture God.

And we do that by beginning to see Christ's face in the faces of the people around us, not the institutions. Christ lives under the bridges of this city. Christ begs for food on the streets. Yet Christ also works in the mayor's office. Sometimes he even drives a Lexus.

We come to see at Christmas that we are all reflections of the God of life, all sisters and brothers of Jesus Christ. And realizing that, we begin treating others with the same dignity we would treat our Lord himself.

When we understand this in the depths of our being, we have peace, at least its beginnings. And if we can allow peace to begin with us, who knows where it will end?

On the Edge

Living on the edge isn't easy, yet that's where most of us live. I write these words on the edge of a new year. You perhaps read them on the edge of new realities in your life. The unknown that looms ahead may be promising or foreboding, perhaps both, yet the fact that it is unknown represents an eternal edge in life. We live on the edge. Oftentimes it boils down simply to that.

Living on the edge is our fate as Christians, also. Since Christ came, we reside in two worlds. We live in this present world, filled as it is with pain, suffering, selfishness, and sin. We live in a world where the innocent suffer, where the weak are often trampled, and where might too often makes right. We live in a world where we all too easily judge the motives of others without giving a thought to our own. This seems to be the human condition.

And yet, as disciples of Christ, our "citizenship" is not in this present world. Our home is the kingdom of God. And in that kingdom, sin is no more. Sorrow and sighing are banished. Death's power is broken. God's love is all in all, and peace is the rule, not the exception.

We saw the dawning of that world in the life and ministry of Jesus. When his Spirit breaks down the barriers in our hearts and we live his principles, we can even see the beginnings of it in the church. It is present in our world, if as yet unrealized, and ironically enough, suffering often makes us more clearly aware of it.

And yet, we're not quite there. We're still on the edge. As the old gospel hymn says, "By faith we can see it afar." Sometimes, though, seeing it "afar" just doesn't seem to be enough, and we ask the question the prophets of old asked: "How long, O Lord?"

How long, Lord, until the hungry are fed? How long until the bullets no longer fly on our streets? How long until the homeless are housed? How long, not necessarily until the "lamb and lion lie down together," but until black and white, straight and gay, rich and poor, can live in peace? How long until we judge not others but ourselves by a Christly standard and leave the judgment of the world to God? How long until "thy will be done on earth as it is in heaven"?

It seems like a long time, sometimes. We tire of the edge, sometimes. And yet as the New Year dawns, keep in mind that there are worse things than the edge. Those of us who live between the "already" of Christ's advent and the "not yet" of his kingdom's glory do well to remember that it is better to see the coming world "afar" than not to see it at all. It is better to suffer the darkness before the dawn than to live in the darkness without dawn. It is better to anticipate what lies ahead, to live on the edge, than to live in edgeless emptiness and evil.

So, as the New Year dawns, let us take comfort and hope in the New Day that by God's grace will come. Let us hold fast, let us share Christ's love, let us rejoice—even in the face of suffering. By faith we can see it afar—and that's enough for now.

Happy New Year.

JUST A LITTLE BOY...

Epiphany is a fancy Greek word that the dictionaries tell us means "manifestation." Something hidden, something wondrous, makes itself known, in other words. We see it clearly where before perhaps we had seen it only dimly or not at all. Epiphany is the farther side of what Paul described when he said, "Now we see in a mirror dimly, but then we will see face to face. Now I know only in part; then I will know fully, even as I have been fully known" (1 Corinthians 13:12).

The ancient churches celebrated this Sunday twelve days after Christmas as Epiphany Sunday. They commemorated through it the visit of the wise men to the infant Jesus, the first manifestation of God's Savior to the Gentiles. Gentiles, of course, are folks like us. I have marveled lately at this story of the wise men: how they undertook their arduous, midwinter journey out of childlike faith, yet responded to murderous King Herod with a worldly shrewdness that saved Jesus' life. What must have passed through their minds when they beheld, perhaps even held, the infant Messiah?

Lightnin' Hopkins, a blues musician, told a story that sheds some light on it for me. Hopkins built himself a guitar out of a cigar box and bailing wire when he was eight years old. His rough-hewn musical genius quickly manifested itself. One day with homemade guitar in hand, little Hopkins ran across Blind Lemon Jefferson, another great blues musician, at a county fair. Jefferson played. Little boy Hopkins played, too. The crowd, who could see Hopkins, was astonished, but not as astonished as Jefferson, who had no idea the person playing along with him was only eight.

"Who's that playing that guitar?" Jefferson asked.

"It's just a little old boy knocking on his guitar," someone in the crowd answered.

"No," Jefferson insisted, "he's *playing* that guitar! Come here, boy."

Hopkins slouched over shyly, as eight-year-olds are inclined to do. Jefferson reached out his old blind hands, felt the child's tiny size, and rocked back in amazement.

"This here was playing that guitar?" the old man shouted in surprise. How could such a big sound come from such a small child?

So, I imagine, the wise men felt when they took the infant Jesus in their arms. Wrapped in swaddling clothes, eyes tightly shut in sleep, little baby sighs and helplessness...so tiny, so vulnerable.

"This here's gonna save the world?" they probably whispered in amazement. "This here?" Yet just as Jefferson knew from the boy's playing what caliber of genius he was, the wise men knew from the utter awe in their hearts what kind of Messiah God had sent. So God's wonder manifested itself to the Gentiles for the very first time.

It still does, of course. May our wondering hearts be open to it.